Study Guide for use with

Business
A Changing World

First Canadian Edition

O.C. Ferrell
Colorado State University

Geoffrey Hirt
DePaul University

Rick Bates
University of Guelph

Elliott Currie
University of Guelph

Prepared by
Peter Mombourquette
Mount Saint Vincent University

Toronto Montréal Boston Burr Ridge, IL Dubuque, IA Madison, WI New York San Francisco
St. Louis Bangkok Bogotá Caracas Kuala Lumpur Lisbon London Madrid
Mexico City Milan New Delhi Santiago Seoul Singapore Sydney Taipei

McGraw-Hill
Ryerson Limited

A Subsidiary of The McGraw-Hill Companies

Study Guide for use with
Business: A Changing World
First Canadian Edition

ISBN: 0-07-091724-8

1 2 3 4 5 6 7 8 9 10 CP 0 9 8 7 6 5 4 3

Printed and bound in Canada.

Care has been taken to trace ownership of copyright material contained in this text; however, the publisher will welcome any information that enables them to rectify any reference or credit for subsequent editions.

Vice President and Editorial Director: Patrick Ferrier
Sponsoring Editor: Lenore Gray Spence
Managing Editor, Development: Kim Brewster
Production Coordinator: Madeleine Harrington
Printer: Canadian Printco

Ferrell, Hirt, Bates, Currie, Business: A Changing World, First Edition

TABLE OF CONTENTS

Chapter 1 The Dynamics of Business and Economics

CHAPTER OUTLINE

Introduction

CHAPTER OBJECTIVES

After reading this chapter, you will be able to:
- Define basic concepts such as business, product, and profit, and explain why studying business is important.
- Identify the main participants and activities of business.
- Define economics and compare the four types of economic systems.
- Describe the role of supply, demand, and competition in a free-enterprise system.
- Specify how and why the health of the economy is measured.
- Trace the evolution of the Canadian economy and discuss the role of the entrepreneur in the economy.
- Evaluate a small-business owner's situation and propose a course of action.

CHAPTER RECAP

THE NATURE OF BUSINESS

A business is an individual or organization that tries to earn a profit by providing products that satisfy people's needs. The outcome of a business's efforts is a product, a good, or service that has both tangible and intangible characteristics that provide satisfaction and benefits. Most people associate the word *product* with tangible goods, such as an automobile, but a product can also be a service, which results when people or machines provide or process something of value to customers, or an idea, such as a solution to a problem.

Chapter 1 The Dynamics of Business and Economics

The primary goal of all businesses is to earn a profit, the difference between what it costs to make and sell a product and what a customer pays for it. Businesses have the right to keep and use their profits as they choose--within legal limits--because profit is the reward for the risks they take in providing products. Not all organizations are businesses: Nonprofit organizations may provide goods and/or services but do not have the fundamental purpose of earning profits.

To earn a profit, a business needs management skills to plan, organize, and control its activities and to find and develop employees so that it can make products that consumers will buy. It needs marketing expertise to determine what products consumers need and want, and to develop, manufacture, price, promote, and distribute those products. It also needs financial resources and skills to fund, maintain, and expand its operations. Businesspeople must abide by laws and regulations; act in a socially responsible manner; and adapt to economic, technological, and social changes. All organizations, even those without a profit objective, engage in management, marketing, and finance activities to help reach their goals.

Figure 1.1 showed the people and activities involved in business. Owners put up the resources--money or credit--to start a business. Employees are responsible for the work that goes on within a business. Owners can manage the business themselves or hire managers to accomplish its tasks. A business's major role is to satisfy its customers. Figure 1.1 also indicated that forces beyond an organization's control--such as government and legal forces, the economy, competition, and ethical and social concerns--all affect operations.

Management involves coordinating employees' actions to achieve the firm's goals; organizing people to work efficiently; motivating them to achieve the business's goals; and acquiring, developing, and using resources effectively and efficiently. In essence, managers plan, organize, staff, and control the tasks required to carry out the work of the company. Marketing includes all the activities designed to provide goods and services that satisfy consumers' needs and wants. Marketers gather information to determine what customers want and then use promotion--advertising, personal selling, sales promotion, and publicity--to communicate the benefits and advantages of their products. Finance refers to activities concerned with obtaining money and using it effectively.

Business is important because it provides both employment for most people and the vast majority of products consumers need to survive and enjoy life. Additionally, business activities and skills occur in nonprofit organizations. Learning about business can help you be a well-informed member of society.

THE ECONOMIC FOUNDATIONS OF BUSINESS

Economics is the study of how resources are distributed for the production of goods and services within a social system. Land, forests, minerals, water, and other things that are not made by people are **natural resources. Human resources**, or labour, refers to the physical and mental abilities that people use to produce goods and services. **Financial resources**, or capital, are the funds used to acquire the natural and human resources needed to provide products. These resources are also called factors *of production* because they are used to make goods and services.

An **economic system** describes how a particular society distributes its resources to produce goods and services. Economic systems handle the distribution of resources in different ways, but all economic systems must address three important issues: (1) What goods and services and how much of each will satisfy consumers' needs? (2) How will goods and services be produced, and who will produce them

Chapter 1 The Dynamics of Business and Economics

and with what resources? and (3) How are the goods and services to be distributed to consumers? The basic economic systems found in the world today--communism, socialism, and capitalism--have fundamental differences in the way they address these issues.

Communism was first described by Karl Marx as an economic system in which the people, without regard to class, own all the nation's resources. In a communist economy, central government planning determines what goods and services will satisfy citizens' needs, how the goods and services will be produced, and how they will be distributed. **Socialism** is an economic system in which the government owns and operates basic industries, but individuals own most of the other businesses. Central government planning determines the answers to the three economic questions for basic products; the forces of supply and demand govern for other products. **Capitalism**, or **free enterprise**, is an economic system in which individuals own and operate the majority of businesses that provide goods and services. Competition, supply, and demand determine the answers to the three basic economic questions. In pure capitalism, or a **free-market system**, all economic decisions are made without government intervention; in modified capitalism, the government intervenes to a certain extent. Most nations operate as **mixed economies**, which have elements of more than one economic system.

Canada and many other countries have economies based on free enterprise, which depends on market demand and supply. For free enterprise to work and motivate participants to succeed, several rights must exist: the right to own private property, the right to earn and use profits, the right to make business decisions within the law, and the right of free choice.

The concepts of supply and demand drive the distribution of resources and products in a free-enterprise system. **Demand** is the number of goods and services that consumers are willing to buy at different prices at a specific time. **Supply** is the number of products that businesses are willing to sell at different prices at a specific time. Both can be shown graphically as supply and demand curves. Where a product's supply and demand curves intersect is the **equilibrium price**, the price at which the number of products that businesses are willing to supply equals the amount of products that consumers are willing to buy at a specific point in time. Supply and demand change constantly in response to changes in economic conditions, availability of resources, and degree of competition. Critics of supply and demand say the system does not distribute resources equally.

Competition, the rivalry among businesses for consumers' dollars, is another vital element in free enterprise. Competition fosters efficiency and low prices by forcing producers to offer the best products at the most reasonable price. There are four types of competitive environments. **Pure competition** exists when there are many small businesses selling one standardized product, such as agricultural commodities like wheat and cotton. Producers cannot differentiate their products, so prices are determined by supply and demand. **Monopolistic competition** exists when there are fewer businesses than in a pure-competition environment and the differences among the goods they sell are small. Businesses have some power over the price they charge because they can make consumers aware of product differences through advertising. An **oligopoly** exists when there are very few businesses selling a product. Nonetheless, the prices charged by different firms stay fairly close because a price cut or increase by one company will usually be matched by its competitors. A **monopoly** exists when there is just one business providing a product in a given market. Monopolies include government-regulated utilities and businesses that hold patents for a specified number of years.

Chapter 1 The Dynamics of Business and Economics

Economies experience cycles of expansion and contraction, often in response to changes in consumer, business, and government spending, as well as war or natural disaster. **Economic expansion** occurs when an economy is growing and people are spending more money; their purchases stimulate the production of goods and services, which in turn spurs employment. However, rapid expansions of the economy may result in **inflation**, a continuing rise in prices. **Economic contraction** occurs when spending declines. Businesses cut back on production and lay off workers, slowing down economic growth. Contractions lead to **recession**--a decline in production, employment, and income. Unemployment refers to the percentage of the population that wants to work but is unable to find jobs. A severe recession can become a **depression**, in which unemployment is very high, consumer spending is low, and business output is sharply reduced.

Countries measure the state of their economies to determine whether they are expanding or contracting and if corrective action is necessary to minimize the fluctuations. One common measure is **gross domestic product (GDP)**--the sum of all goods and services produced in a country during a year. GDP measures only those goods and services made within a country and therefore does not include profits from companies' overseas operations; it does include profits earned by foreign companies within the country being measured. Another important indicator of a nation's economic health is the relationship between its spending and income (from taxes). When a nation spends more than it takes in from taxes, it has a **budget deficit**. The United States has run a budget deficit for many years.

THE CANADIAN ECONOMY

Canada is a mixed economy based on free enterprise. The answers to the three economic questions are determined by competition, supply, and demand, although the federal government intervenes in economic decisions to a certain extent.

Canada's early economic activity focused on Atlantic Canadian fisheries and fur trading. As settlements continued to grow, forestry and farming emerged to compliment the two main industries. The 19th century saw the birth of a National railway and the Industrial Revolution. The railway allowed farmers to send crops and goods to urban areas and pushed settlements westward leading to major growth in agriculture. The Industrial Revolution brought about new technologies and the development of factories, in which work was specialized. Central Canada jumped to the forefront as the manufacturing centre of Canada with factories producing a variety of goods including steel, farm equipment and alcohol. The remainder of the country, while experiencing some aspects of Industrialization, remained primarily agrarian.

The Canadian economy continued to grow and prosper during the early 20th century due to industrialization and growth in agriculture and resource-based industries. After World War II, Canada's economy slowly began to change from heavy dependence on natural resources to a focus on providing services for the growing, prosperous population. During the later half of the century Canadians achieved a very high standard of living, and the nation gradually became a service economy -- one devoted to the production of services that made life easier for consumers.

An **entrepreneur** is an individual who risks his or her wealth, time, and effort to develop for profit an innovative product or way of doing something. The free-enterprise system provides the conditions necessary for entrepreneurs to succeed. Entrepreneurs are constantly changing Canadian business practices with new technology and innovative management techniques.

Chapter 1 The Dynamics of Business and Economics

The Canadian economic system is best described as modified capitalism because the federal (as well as provincial and municipal) government regulates business to a certain extent to preserve competition and protect consumers, employees, and the environment. Additionally, government agencies such as the Department of Finance and the Bank of Canada measure the health of the economy and, when necessary, take steps to minimize the disruptive effects of economic fluctuations and reduce unemployment.

CAN YOU LEARN BUSINESS IN A CLASSROOM?

To be successful in business, you need knowledge, experience, skills, and good judgment. This book will help you gain some of the knowledge you need. The examples, boxes, and case within each chapter describe experiences to help you develop good business judgment. Skill-building exercises and dilemmas will help you develop skills that may be useful in your future career. Good judgment is based on knowledge, experience, personal insight, and understanding, so you'll need more courses in business, along with some practical experience, to help you develop the special insight necessary to put your personal stamp on knowledge as you apply it.

ENHANCEMENT EXERCISES

1. The chapter spends a great deal of time discussing the role and importance of entrepreneurs in Canada's economic system. Have you ever practiced entrepreneurship? Do you think you would enjoy the challenges? A simple entrepreneurship exercise is to start a business for a day or two with a minimal investment. Select a business that you are interested in, either alone or in a small group, and start the business with only one dollar. You may use any materials or goods that you already own but cannot spend more than one dollar.

Prior to starting, write out a simple plan noting whom your customers will be and how you will let them know about your product or service. After running the business count up the money and record what worked well, what you would do differently and whether or not you enjoyed the experience.

By completing this exercise not only will you have experienced the thrill of entrepreneurship, but you will also have written a business plan!

If you are stuck for ideas, some easy businesses are tie-dying T-shirts, pre-selling sandwiches, cleaning rooms, washing cars, etc. You are limited only by your imagination.

2. Perhaps running a business for a day was not enough. If you really want to learn what it is like to run a business interview several local entrepreneurs. Alone or in a small group, compile a list of questions and contact several business owners for answers. Your questions are limited only by your imagination. But remember to ask the most important question – "What is good business to start in the future?" You may just discover an idea that enables you to be the next Armand Bombardier or KC Irving.

Chapter 1 The Dynamics of Business and Economics

MATCHING QUIZ

Match the following key terms with the correct definition.

a. communism
b. socialism
c. capitalism
d. demand
e. supply

_____1.   An economic system in which individuals own and operate the majority of businesses that provide goods and services.

_____2.   A society in which the people, without regard to class, own all the nation's resources.

_____3.   The number of products that businesses are willing to sell at different prices at a specific time.

_____4.   An economic system in which the government owns and operates basic industries, but individuals own most businesses.

_____5.   The number of goods and services that consumers are willing to buy at different prices at a specific time.

TRUE/FALSE QUIZ

Indicate whether each of the following statements is true or false.

_____1.   A product is a good.

_____2.   Under socialism, the forces of supply and demand determine what goods and services will be produced and how and by whom they will be produced.

_____3.   Business involves profit-seeking activities that provide products that satisfy people's needs

_____4.   Marketing involves coordinating employees' actions to achieve the firm's goals, organizing people to work efficiently, and motivating them to achieve the business's goals.

_____5.   Canada practices pure capitalism.

_____6.   Businesses have the right to keep and use profits as they choose, within legal limits.

_____7.   Critics of supply and demand claim that it is unfair because the wealthy can afford to buy more than they need, but the poor are unable to buy enough of what they need.

Ferrell, Hirt, Bates & Currie, Business: A Changing World, First Edition

Chapter 1 The Dynamics of Business and Economics

_____ 8.   Gross domestic product is the sum of all goods and services produced in a country during a year.

_____ 9.   When the economy is contracting, the federal government may increase its spending for goods and services to stimulate growth.

_____ 10.   John W. Billes, Alfred Billes and Armand Bombardier founded Canadian Tire.

_____ 11.   Supply is the number of goods and services that consumers are willing to buy at different prices at a specific time.

_____ 12.   Under pure capitalism, or laissez-faire capitalism, the government regulates businesses.

_____ 13.   If the price of cotton goes up because of drought, the equilibrium price of 100-percent cotton T-shirts will rise because sellers will offer more shirts for sale at the old equilibrium price.

_____ 14.   Inflation is a decline in production, employment, and income.

_____ 15.   When a nation spends more than it takes in from taxes, it has a budget deficit.

_____ 16.   An economic system determines what products and how many will satisfy society, how and who will produce those products and with what resources, and how products will be distributed to consumers.

_____ 17.   It is the managers' primary responsibility to provide financial resources for the operation of the business.

_____ 18.   Sellers in a pure-competition environment can control their prices because they can promote their products as being different from others.

_____ 19.   Canada's most prominent entrepreneurs are KC Irving, Armand Bombardier and Michael Dell.

_____ 20.   Nonprofit organizations, although they may provide a good or service, do not have the fundamental purpose of earning profits.

MULTIPLE-CHOICE QUIZ

Choose the correct answer for each of the following questions.

_____ 1.   Which of the following is characterized by few businesses selling a product?
a.   pure competition
b.   monopolistic competition
c.   dualistic competition
d.   oligopoly
e.   monopoly

Chapter 1 The Dynamics of Business and Economics

_____2.	When you purchase a product, what you are actually buying is (are)
	a.	a good.
	b.	a service.
	c.	an idea.
	d.	a profit.
	e.	the benefits and satisfaction you think the product will provide.

_____3.	Which of the following describes the Canadian economy before the Industrial Revolution?
	a.	service economy
	b.	agricultural economy
	c.	manufacturing economy
	d.	factory economy
	e.	no economy

_____4.	In which of the following systems does central government planning and, to a certain extent, the forces of supply and demand determine what goods and services will be produced?
	a.	communism
	b.	pure competition
	c.	modified capitalism
	d.	pure capitalism
	e.	socialism

_____5.	The primary goal of business is to
	a.	earn a profit.
	b.	sell a product.
	c.	be ethical.
	d.	manage people.
	e.	beat the competition.

_____6.	Activities designed to provide products that satisfy customers are known as
	a.	finance.
	b.	marketing.
	c.	management.
	d.	advertising.
	e.	manufacturing.

_____7.	The physical and mental abilities that people use to produce goods and services are called
	a.	natural resources.
	b.	human resources.
	c.	mortal resources.
	d.	financial resources.
	e.	work.

Chapter 1 The Dynamics of Business and Economics

____8.   Which of the following currently describes the Canadian economy?
   a.   entrepreneurial economy
   b.   free-for-all economy
   c.   agricultural economy
   d.   manufacturing economy
   e.   service and Internet-based economy

____9.   Under which of the following do supply and demand have the greatest influence?
   a.   communism
   b.   socialism
   c.   capitalism
   d.   modified communism
   e.   mixed economy

____10.   Which of the following is a measure of the sum of all goods and services produced by a nation in one year?
   a.   gross product
   b.   gross domestic product
   c.   budget deficit
   d.   real gross domestic product
   e.   real gross national product

____11.   Which of the following best describes the economic system of Canada?
   a.   free-market system
   b.   pure capitalism
   c.   laissez-faire capitalism
   d.   modified capitalism
   e.   socialism

____12.   The activity concerned with coordinating employees' actions to achieve the firm's goals, organizing people to work efficiently, and motivating them to achieve the business's goals is called
   a.   finance.
   b.   marketing.
   c.   management.
   d.   leading.
   e.   dictating.

____13.   A negative relationship between a nation's spending and income is called a
   a.   loss.
   b.   trade deficit.
   c.   budget deficit.
   d.   product deficit.
   e.   global deficit.

Chapter 1 The Dynamics of Business and Economics

_____14.   A decline in production, employment, and income is called
        a. recession.
        b. depression.
        c. economic expansion.
        d. unemployment.
        inflation.

SKILL-BUILDING QUIZ

After completing the "Build Your Skills" exercise, you should be able to choose the correct answer for each of the following questions.

_____1.   After plotting the supply and demand curves for WagWumps, specify which of the following is the equilibrium price:
        a. $26.99
        b. $23.99
        c. $22.99
        d. $21.99

_____2.   If WagWumps are shown in a successful children's film, what do you think will happen to demand for the WagWumps toy?
        a. Demand will go down.
        b. Demand will go up.
        c. Demand will remain the same.
        d. Supply will go down.

_____3.   If Wee-Toys' costs of making WagWumps suddenly increase, the number it is willing to supply will likely fall. If demand remains the same, what will happen to the equilibrium price?
        a. Nothing, it will stay the same.
        b. It will quadruple.
        c. It will fall.
        d. It will rise.

_____4.   If Wee-Toys announces that it will stop making and selling WagWumps on a certain future date, which of the following do you think will happen?
        a. The equilibrium price will increase as customers rush to grab the last toys.
        b. The equilibrium price will decrease as customers rush to grab the last toys.
        c. The equilibrium price will remain the same because there will be no change in supply or demand.
        d. The market for WagWumps will immediately collapse.

Chapter 1 The Dynamics of Business and Economics

ANSWERS

MATCHING QUIZ

1. c   2. a   3. e   4. b   5. d

TRUE/FALSE QUIZ

1. F	5. F	9. T	13. F	17. F
2. F	6. T	10. T	14. F	18. F
3. T	7. T	11. F	15. T	19. F
4. F	8. T	12. F	16. T	20. T

MULTIPLE-CHOICE QUIZ

1. d	4. e	7. b	10. e	13. c
2. e	5. a	8. e	11. d	14. a
3. b	6. b	9. c	12. c	

SKILL-BUILDING QUIZ

1. c   2. b   3. d   4. a

Chapter 2 The Legal and Regulatory Environment

CHAPTER OUTLINE

Introduction

Sources of Law

Courts and the Resolution of Disputes
    The Court System
    Alternative Dispute Resolution Methods

Administrative Tribunals

Important Elements of Business Law
    The Sale of Good Act
    The Law of Torts and Fraud
    The Law of Contracts
    The Law of Agency
    The Law of Property
    The Law of Bankruptcy

The Internet: Legal and Regulatory Issues

Legal Pressure for Responsible Business Conduct

CHAPTER OBJECTIVES

After reading this chapter, you should be able to:

- Identify the sources of law.
- Summarize the court system and the methods of conflict resolution.
- Gain an appreciation of the framework for regulating business through administrative agencies.
- Review important elements of business law, including the Sale of Goods Act, the law of torts and fraud, the law of contracts, the law of agency, the law of property, and the law of bankruptcy.
- Review the legal and regulatory implications of electronic business.
- Provide an overview of the legal pressure for responsible business conduct.
- Identify the legal issues in a business dispute.

Chapter 2 The Legal and Regulatory Environment

CHAPTER RECAP

SOURCES OF LAW

Business law refers to the rules and regulations that govern the conduct of business. Problems in this area come from the failure to keep promises, misunderstandings, disagreements about expectations, or attempts to take advantage of others. The regulatory environment offers a framework and enforcement system in order to provide a fair playing field for all businesses. Examining business law and the regulatory environment will allow you to see the importance of this area and also make you aware of your rights in the business world.

Laws are classified as either criminal or civil. Criminal law not only prohibits a specific kind of action but also imposes a fine or imprisonment as punishment for violating the law. Civil law defines all the laws not classified as criminal, and it specifies the rights and duties of individuals and organizations. Violations of civil law may result in fines but not imprisonment.

Laws are derived from four sources: the Constitution (the Canadian Charter of Rights and Freedoms), precedents established by judges (common law), federal and provincial statutes (statute law), and federal and provincial administrative agencies (administrative law).

COURTS AND THE RESOLUTION OF DISPUTES

The primary method of conflict resolution and business disputes is through **lawsuits** (dispute resolution procedures in which one individual or organization takes another to court). Most business lawsuits involve a request for a sum of money, but some lawsuits request that a court specifically order a person or organization to do or to refrain from doing a certain act.

The legal system provides a forum for resolving disputes. **Jurisdiction** is the legal power of a court to interpret and apply the law and make a binding decision. A **trial court** determines the facts of a case, decides which laws pertain, and applies those laws to resolve the dispute. An **appellate court** deals solely with appeals relating to the interpretation of the law.

Alternative dispute resolution methods are becoming popular because of the crowded schedules of state and federal trial courts and the expense involved in complex cases. **Mediation** is a form of negotiation to resolve a dispute by bringing in one or more third parties, usually chosen by the disputing parties, to help reach a settlement. The mediator's resolution is nonbinding. **Arbitration** involves submission of a dispute to one or more third parties, usually chosen by the disputing parties, whose decision is final.

ADMINISTRATIVE TRIBUNALS

Federal and provincial administrative tribunals also have some judicial powers, and many decide disputes involving their regulations. For example, The Federal Competition Act and Competition Tribunal Act of 1986 have established our competition tribunal. Its purpose is to ensure fair competition exists for the betterment of the Canadian economy. Appeals of federal tribunal ruling proceed to federal court while provincial appeals either go to the court system or to the provincial cabinet in question.

Chapter 2 The Legal and Regulatory Environment

IMPORTANT ELEMENTS OF BUSINESS LAW

To avoid violating criminal and civil laws and to prevent lawsuits, business people should be familiar with laws that address business practices: laws relating to sales, contracts, agents, property, and competition. The **Sale of Goods Act**, a set of laws covering several business law topics, was enacted to simplify commerce. The act covers sales agreements for goods and services but does not cover the sale of stocks and bonds, personal services, or real estate. The act requires that for a sale to occur there must be a payment of money for the goods, so in the case of barter the act does not apply.

A **tort** is a private or civil wrong other than breach of contract. **Fraud** is a purposeful unlawful act to deceive or manipulate in order to damage others. An important aspect of tort law involves **product liability**--businesses' legal responsibility for any negligence in the design, production, sale, and consumption of products.

Virtually every business transaction is carried out by means of a **contract**, a mutual agreement between two or more parties that can be enforced in a court if one party chooses not to comply with the terms. Only contracts that meet certain requirements (elements) are enforceable by the courts. The requirements are voluntary agreement, consideration, contractual capacity, and legality. **Breach of contract** is the failure or refusal of a party to a contract to live up to his or her promises.

An **agency** is a common business relationship created when one person acts on behalf of another and under that person's control. Two parties are involved in an agency relationship: the **principal** is the one who wishes to have a specific task accomplished and the **agent** is the one who acts on behalf of the principal to accomplish the task.

Property law is broad in scope because it covers the ownership and transfer of all kinds of property. **Real property** consists of real estate and everything permanently attached to it. **Personal property** basically is everything else. **Intellectual property** refers to property, such as musical works, artwork, books, and computer software, that is generated by a person's creative activities. Copyrights, patents, and trademarks provide protection to the owners of property by giving them the exclusive right to use it.

Although few businesses and individuals intentionally fail to repay their debts, sometimes they cannot fulfill their financial obligations. An option of last resort in these cases is **bankruptcy**, or legal insolvency. Under the Canadian Bankruptcy and Insolvency Act, a person or company may be insolvent because they are not able to pay creditors.

THE INTERNET: LEGAL AND REGULATORY ISSUES

Business use and dependence on the Internet is increasingly creating potential legal problems. There are few specific laws that regulate business on the Internet, but the standards for acceptable behaviour that are reflected in basic laws and regulations designed for traditional businesses can be applied to business on the Internet as well. The central focus for future legislation of business conducted on the Internet is the protection of personal privacy. The first strides toward regulating Internet commerce are emerging in Europe.

Chapter 2 The Legal and Regulatory Environment

ENHANCEMENT EXERCISES

1. Several companies have complained about Air Canada and its pricing policies in the last few years. Competitors such as CanJet and Canada 3000 have argued in the press and before the Competition tribunal that the airline is trying to monopolize the airline industry by lowering its prices on routes that new airlines are flying while maintaining high prices on similar routes with no competition. Through the use of the Internet, business journals and other available sources, compile a scrapbook of information on the subject. Afterwards, answer the one or more of the following questions:
   a) Is Air Canada trying to monopolize the Canadian air market?
   b) Should the government intervene?
   c) What problems could occur if Air Canada became the only option for Canadians?

MATCHING QUIZ

Match the following key terms with the correct definition.

a. mediation
b. trial court
c. arbitration
d. tort
e. appellate court

_____1.   Settlement of a labor/management dispute by a third party whose solution is legally binding and enforceable.

_____2.   A court that deals solely with appeals relating to the interpretation of law.

_____3.   A wrong to another or their property or their reputation.

_____4.   A form of negotiation to resolve a dispute by bringing in one or more third-parties to help reach a settlement.

_____5.   A court that determines the facts of a case, decides which laws pertain, and applies those laws to resolve the dispute.

TRUE/FALSE QUIZ

Indicate whether each of the following statements is true or false.

_____1.   The federal Competition Act and the Competition Tribunal Act maintain and encourage competition in Canada.

_____2.   Jurisdiction is the legal power of a court, through a judge, to interpret and apply the law and make a binding decision in a particular case.

Chapter 2 The Legal and Regulatory Environment

_____3.   Arbitration involves submission of a dispute to one or more third-party arbitrators, usually chosen by the disputing parties whose decision is final barring appeal.

_____4.   In an agency relationship, the party who wishes to have a specific task accomplished is known as the agent.

_____5.   Lawsuits are the primary method of resolving conflicts and business disputes.

_____6.   Common law is derived from common sense.

_____7.   Breach of contract can be a tort.

_____8.   Bankruptcy is automatically granted if a business cannot pay its creditors.

_____9.   The purpose of the Sales of Goods Act was to simplify commerce.

_____10.   The Sales of Goods Act covers the barter of items.

_____11.   Europe is not concerned about implementing Internet rules and regulations.

_____12.   Laws concerning the Internet are widely known and understood.

_____13.   Canada has enacted the Uniform Commercial Code.

_____14.   A "handshake deal" is in most cases as fully and completely binding as a written, signed contract.

_____15.   One requirement for enforcement of a contract is that it must be supported by consideration.

_____16.   Violations of criminal law may result in fines but not imprisonment.

_____17.   Intellectual property refers to property, such as musical works and artwork, that is generated by a person's creative activities.

_____18.   The Competition Act is no longer relevant in today's changing world.

_____19.   The central focus for future legislation of business conducted on the Internet is the protection of personal privacy.

_____20.   Criminal and civil laws are derived from seven sources.

Chapter 2 The Legal and Regulatory Environment

MULTIPLE-CHOICE QUIZ

Choose the correct answer for each of the following questions.

_____1.   What kind of property consists of rights and duties?
   a.   intellectual
   b.   personal
   c.   real
   d.   intangible
   e.   tangible

_____2.   Which of the following is an example of tangible property?
   a.   accounts receivable
   b.   goodwill
   c.   trademarks
   d.   stock in a corporation
   e.   business inventory

_____3.   The central focus for future legislation of business conducted on the Internet is
   a.   fair pricing.
   b.   good selection.
   c.   personal privacy.
   d.   acceptable communications.
   e.   faster service.

_____4.   What is the name given to people who attempt to sell back the registration of matching Internet sites to the trademark owner?
   a.   cyber-squatters
   b.   hackers
   c.   cyber-hackers
   d.   cyber-thieves
   e.   squatters

_____5.   In which kind of court are cases reevaluated but not retried?
   a.   trial court
   b.   private court
   c.   appellate court
   d.   jurisdiction court
   e.   mediation court

_____6.   _____ protect the ownership rights on material such as books, music, videos, photos, and computer software.
   a.   Copyrights
   b.   Intellectual property rights
   c.   Personal property rights
   d.   Real property laws
   e.   Trademarks

Chapter 2 The Legal and Regulatory Environment

_____7.   Which of the following contracts is required by most states to be in writing?
   a.   contracts involving the sale of land
   b.   contracts to pay somebody else's debt
   c.   contracts that cannot be fulfilled within one year
   d.   contracts for the sale of goods that cost more than $500
   e.   all of the above

_____8.   McDonald's golden arches are an example of
   a.   a patent.
   b.   a copyright.
   c.   a trademark.
   d.   intellectual property.
   e.   intangible property.

SKILL-BUILDING QUIZ

In the "Build Your Skills" exercise in Chapter 2, you learned that large organizations can get into trouble with the government through fraud. Keeping this in mind, choose the best answers for the following.

_____1.   If Columbia/HCA made a mistake in billing the government, _____ would result.
   a.   fraud
   b.   the need for self-reporting and correction of the error
   c.   product liability
   d.   a tort related to pricing a health care product
   e.   a civil wrong

_____2.   If Columbia/HCA was purposeful in manipulating pricing to overcharge the government, it would result in
   a.   fraud.
   b.   the need for self-reporting and correction of the error.
   c.   product liability.
   d.   a tort related to pricing a health care product.
   e.   a civil wrong.

_____3.   In the case of Columbia/HCA both the _____ and the organization are accountable for criminal conduct.
   a.   government
   b.   individual employees
   c.   FBI
   d.   Medicare program
   e.   consumers

Chapter 2 The Legal and Regulatory Environment

ANSWERS

MATCHING QUIZ

1. c   2. e   3. d   4. a   5. b

TRUE/FALSE QUIZ

1. T	5. T	9. T	13. F	17. T
2. T	6. F	10. F	14. T	18. F
3. F	7. F	11. F	15. T	19. T
4. F	8. F	12. F	16. F	20. F

MULTIPLE-CHOICE QUIZ

1. d	4. a	7. e
2. e	5. c	8. c
3. c	6. a	

SKILL-BUILDING QUIZ

1. b   2. a   3. b

Chapter 3 Business Ethics and Social Responsibility

CHAPTER OBJECTIVES

After reading this chapter, you should be able to:
- Define business ethics and examine its importance.
- Detect some of the ethical issues that may arise in business.
- Specify how businesses can improve ethical behaviour.
- Define social responsibility and explain its relevance to business.
- Debate an organization's social responsibilities to owners, employees, consumers, the environment, and the community.
- Evaluate the ethics of a business's decision.

CHAPTER RECAP

BUSINESS ETHICS AND SOCIAL RESPONSIBILITY

Business ethics refers to principles and standards that define acceptable conduct in the world of business. The acceptability of behaviour in business is determined by customers, competitors, government regulators, interest groups, and the public, as well as by each individual's personal moral principles and values. Social responsibility is a business's obligation to maximize its positive impact and minimize its negative impact on society. Although they are often used interchangeably, the terms *social responsibility* and *ethics* do not mean the same thing. Business ethics relates to an *individual's* or *work group's* decisions that society evaluates as right or wrong; social responsibility is a broader concept that concerns the impact of an *entire business's* activities on society. The most basic ethical and responsibility concerns have been codified as laws and regulations that encourage businesses to

Chapter 3 Business Ethics and Social Responsibility

conform to society's standards, values, and attitudes. Business ethics, social responsibility and laws together act as a compliance system that requires that businesses and employees act responsibly in society.

THE ROLE OF ETHICS IN BUSINESS

Your superiors, coworkers, and family will make judgments about the ethics of your actions and decisions. Learning how to recognize and resolve ethical issues is a crucial step in evaluating ethical decisions in business. It is important to realize that business ethics goes beyond legal issues. Ethical conduct builds trust among individuals and in business relationships, which validates and promotes confidence in business relationships. Well-publicized incidents of unethical activity strengthen the public's perception that ethical standards and the level of trust in business need to be raised.

RECOGNIZING ETHICAL ISSUES IN BUSINESS

Learning to recognize ethical issues is the most important step in understanding business ethics. An **ethical issue** is an identifiable problem, situation, or opportunity that requires a person or organization to choose from among several actions that may be evaluated as right or wrong, ethical or unethical. The best way to judge the ethics of a decision is to look at it from a customer or competitor's viewpoint. Although many business issues seem straightforward and easy to resolve, a person often needs several years of business experience to understand what is acceptable or ethical. Whether an activity is ethical also depends on the culture in which a business operates.

Business ethics issues can be categorized in the context of their relation to conflicts of interest, fairness and honesty, communications, and business associations. A conflict of interest exists when a person must choose whether to advance his or her own personal interests or those of others. **Bribes--**payments, gifts, or special favours intended to influence the outcome of a decision--are one potential source of conflict of interest. Fairness and honesty relate to the general values of decision makers. Businesspersons are expected to obey all applicable laws and regulations and not knowingly to harm customers, clients, or competitors through deception, misrepresentation, or coercion. In the area of communications, false and misleading advertising, deceptive personal selling tactics, lying, and product labeling may be ethical issues. In the area of business relationships, ethical businesspeople strive to keep company secrets, meet obligations and responsibilities, and avoid undue pressure that forces others to behave unethically. **Plagiarism--**taking someone else's work and presenting it as your own--is another issue related to business relationships.

It can be difficult to recognize specific ethical issues in practice. Whether a decision maker recognizes an issue as an ethical one often depends on the issue itself. Open discussion of ethical issues promotes trust and learning.

IMPROVING ETHICAL BEHAVIOUR IN BUSINESS

Understanding how people make ethical choices and what prompts a person to act unethically may reverse the current trend toward unethical behaviour in business. Ethical decisions in an organization are influenced by three factors: individual moral standards, the influence of managers and coworkers, and the opportunity to engage in misconduct. Consequently, the activities and examples set by coworkers, as well as the rules and policies established by the firm, are critical in gaining consistent ethical compliance. It is difficult for employees to determine what conduct is acceptable within a

Chapter 3 Business Ethics and Social Responsibility

company if the firm does not have ethics policies and standards. Professional **codes of ethics** are formalized rules and standards that describe what the company expects of its employees. Codes of ethics, policies on ethics, and ethics training programs advance ethical behaviour because they prescribe which activities are acceptable and which are not, and they limit the opportunity for misconduct by providing punishments for violations of the rules and standards. Enforcement of ethics policies by companies is a common way of dealing with ethical problems. Individuals also play a key role in promoting ethical decisions in the workplace. **Whistleblowing** occurs when an employee exposes an employer's wrongdoing to outsiders, such as the media or government regulatory agencies.

THE NATURE OF SOCIAL RESPONSIBILITY

Social responsibility has four dimensions: economic, legal, ethical, and voluntary (including philanthropic). Earning profits and complying with the law are the first steps of social responsibility. Voluntary responsibilities are additional activities that may not be required but which promote human welfare or goodwill. A business that is concerned about society as well as earning profits is likely to invest voluntarily in socially responsible activities. Companies today view social responsibility as another cost of doing business.

SOCIAL RESPONSIBILITY ISSUES

As with ethics, managers consider social responsibility on a daily basis as they deal with real issues. Among the many social issues that managers must consider are their firm's relations with employees, government regulators, owners, suppliers, customers, and the community.

A business must first be responsible to its owners and investors by striving to maximize their investment in the firm. A business's responsibilities in this area include maintaining proper accounting procedures, providing all relevant information about the current and projected performance of the firm, and protecting the owners' rights and investments.

Employees expect businesses to provide a safe workplace, pay them adequately for their work, tell them what is happening within their company, listen to their grievances, and treat them fairly. Major social responsibility issues in this area relate to safety, compensation, and equality.

Consumerism refers to activities undertaken by independent individuals, groups, and organizations to protect their rights as consumers. Many of their desires were spelled out in John F. Kennedy's 1962 consumer bill of rights, which includes: (1) the right to safety, which means that businesses must not knowingly sell anything that could result in personal injury or harm; (2) the right to be informed, which gives consumers the freedom to review complete information about a product; (3) the right to choose, which gives consumers a variety of products and services at competitive prices; and (4) the right to be heard, which assures consumers that their interests will receive full and sympathetic consideration when the government formulates policy and assures the fair treatment of consumers who voice complaints. Canada uses the rights discussed in Kennedy's speech as a framework to develop policy.

One area of environmental responsibility concerns the rights of animals and the preservation of animal species and their habitats. Other environmental responsibilities deal with pollution. Water pollution results from the dumping of toxic chemicals and sewage into rivers and oceans; the burial of industrial waste in the ground, where it can filter into water supplies, and chemical spills. Air pollution--caused

Chapter 3 Business Ethics and Social Responsibility

by smoke and other pollutants emitted by manufacturing facilities, as well as carbon monoxide and hydrocarbons emitted by motor vehicles--causes acid rain and may contribute to the so-called greenhouse effect. Land pollution issues include deforestation--especially of the rain forests--as well as issues related to waste disposal. Businesses have responded to these issues by trying to eliminate wasteful practices and harmful emissions, reducing packaging, and recycling. Environmental responsibility requires tradeoffs.

A final area of social responsibility concerns businesses' responsibilities to the general welfare of the communities in which they operate. Social responsibility issues in this area relate to charitable contributions to national and local organizations, donations of resources to educational programs, and programs dealing with the hard-core unemployed and homeless.

ENHANCEMENT EXERCISES

1. North America recently experienced a technological bubble on the stock exchange. Companies, especially those that specified in telecommunication and Internet industries, soared in value causing investors to double and triple their money overnight. But as quickly as the stocks rose in value, they declined with some companies going completely out of business. For the following companies, review press releases from the respective Chief Executive Officer's (CEO) on the company websites and read the message from the CEO in the company's annual report for the period 1999-2001.

Compare the press releases of Cisco, Nortel and JDS Uniphase then answer the following questions:
   a) Which of the three companies has acted the most ethically in the past three years when discussing future prospects for business?
   b) What did the respective CEO's get paid? If investors are losing millions should CEO's have their salaries reduced?
   c) If a CEO were to announce business was fine and then report otherwise a short time later, would this be ethical? Do you think such action is criminal?

2. E-Trade is an online brokerage company operating in Canada and the USA. Even though the fortunes of the company have declined significantly, Christos Cotsako's, CEO, saw his salary and bonuses total 21 million dollars for 2001/02.   After receiving pressure from the company's shareholders (owners) Cotsako returned the money and signed a new compensation agreement. Do you think Cotsako should have returned the money?

Search the Internet for other examples of a CEO or other top-level management reducing their salary due to their company's declining fortunes. Are they acting ethically?

MATCHING QUIZ

Match the following key terms with the correct definition.

a.   business ethics
b.   ethical issue
c.   codes of ethics
d.   consumerism
e.   social responsibility

Chapter 3 Business Ethics and Social Responsibility

_____ 1.   An identifiable problem, situation, or opportunity that requires a person to choose from among several actions that may be evaluated as right or wrong, ethical or unethical.

_____ 2.   The principles and standards that determine acceptable conduct in business.

_____ 3.   A business's obligation to maximize its positive impact and minimize its negative impact on society.

_____ 4.   The activities that independent individuals, groups, and organizations undertake to protect their rights as consumers.

_____ 5.   Formalized rules and standards that describe what the company expects of its employees.

TRUE/FALSE QUIZ

Indicate whether each of the following statements is true or false.

_____ 1.   Many ethical issues in business can be categorized in the context of their relation with conflicts of interest, fairness and honesty, communications, and business associations.

_____ 2.   Environmental responsibility imposes costs only on businesses.

_____ 3.   A major social responsibility for business is providing equal opportunities for all employees, regardless of their sex, age, race, religion, or nationality.

_____ 4.   Consumers have a right to review complete information about a product or service before purchasing it.

_____ 5.   Social responsibility is a business's obligation to maximize its negative impact and minimize its positive impact on society.

_____ 6.   Acid rain results when the chemical emissions of manufacturing facilities react with air and rain.

_____ 7.   Consumers have a right to expect products to be safe for their intended use.

_____ 8.   Social responsibility is a passive area of business; the issues never change.

_____ 9.   Plagiarism is taking someone else's work and presenting it as your own.

_____ 10.   Ethics relates to the impact of a business's activities on society.

_____ 11.   The three factors that influence ethical decision making are individual moral standards, the influence of managers and coworkers, and the opportunity to engage in misconduct.

Chapter 3 Business Ethics and Social Responsibility

_____12.   Enforcement of ethics policies is an uncommon way of dealing with ethical problems.

_____13.   It is easy to recognize and deal with an ethical issue.

_____14.   A conflict of interest exists when a person must choose whether to advance his or her own interests or those of others.

_____15.   Codes of ethics, ethics policies, and ethics training programs promote ethical behaviour by prescribing what activities are unacceptable and limiting the opportunity for misconduct by providing punishments for violations of the rules.

_____16.   Plagiarism represents an ethical issue in the category of fairness and honesty.

_____17.   The public, government regulators, interest groups, competitors, and individuals--through their personal morals and values--determine what is ethical.

_____18.   The movement to label music recordings represents an ethical issue because it pits the right of freedom of speech against the rights of parents to protect their children from influences they deem harmful.

_____19.   Whistleblowers are always treated positively.

_____20.   The four dimensions of social responsibility are: economic, legal, ethical, and compulsory.

MULTIPLE-CHOICE QUIZ

Choose the correct answer for each of the following questions.

_____1.   Employees want all the following EXCEPT
   a.   a safe workplace.
   b.   to be paid adequately.
   c.   to have equal opportunities for employment.
   d.   to have their employers listen to their grievances.
   e.   to maximize the owners' investment.

_____2.   According to your text, the best way to judge the ethics of a decision is to look at the situation from the viewpoint of customers or
   a.   government regulators.
   b.   managers.
   c.   employees.
   d.   competitors.
   e.   owners.

_____3.   Which of the following does not contribute to water pollution?
   a.   oil spills

Chapter 3 Business Ethics and Social Responsibility

    b.   carbon monoxide and hydrocarbon emissions
    c.   dumping of toxic chemicals
    d.   burial of industrial wastes in the ground
    e.   dumping of raw sewage into rivers and oceans

_____ 4.   Whistleblowing
    a.   occurs when an employee exposes an employer's wrongdoing to outsiders, such as the media or government regulatory agencies.
    b.   is taking someone else's work and presenting it as your own.
    c.   refers to payments, gifts, or special favors intended to influence the outcome of a decision.
    d.   is a conflict of interest.
    e.   is unethical.

_____ 5.   The fact that consumers have so many different brands of CD players from which to make a selection illustrates
    a.   the right to safety.
    b.   the right to be informed.
    c.   the right to choose.
    d.   the right to be heard.
    e.   none of the above.

_____ 6.   Dealing with the hard-core unemployed is a social responsibility issue in the area of
    a.   relations with owners.
    b.   relations with investors.
    c.   community relations.
    d.   employee relations.
    e.   environmental relations.

_____ 7.   Recycling programs
    a.   reprocess used materials--aluminum, paper, glass, and some plastic--for reuse.
    b.   are mandatory.
    c.   are a waste of time.
    d.   stop air pollution.
    e.   stop noise pollution.

_____ 8.   8. Which of the following MAY contribute to the so-called greenhouse effect?
    a.   land pollution
    b.   water pollution
    c.   noise pollution
    d.   air pollution
    e.   none of the above

_____ 9.   Which of the following is fulfilled by displaying interest-rate information on a charge-card agreement?
    a.   the right to safety
    b.   the right to be informed
    c.   the right to choose

        d. the right to be heard
        e. none of the above

____10.   Which of the following statements about business ethics is FALSE?
        a. Ethical conduct builds trust among individuals and in business relationships.
        b. Ethical violations destroy trust and make it difficult to conduct business.
        c. Business ethics is related to the culture in which a business operates.
        d. Ethical standards in business need to be raised.
        e. Ethical concerns do not change over time.

____11.   Which of the following in NOT part of Kennedy's consumer bill of rights?
        a. the right to safety
        b. the right to choose
        c. the right to be informed
        d. the right to bear arms
        e. the right to be heard

____12.   Which of the following statements about codes of ethics is FALSE?
        a. A code of ethics is a set of formalized rules and standards that describe what a
            company expects of its employees.
        b. Codes of ethics advance ethical behaviour because they prescribe which activities
            are acceptable and which are not, and they limit the opportunity for misconduct by
            providing punishments for violations of the rules and standards.
        c. Without codes of ethics and ethics policies, employees may base decisions on how
            their peers and superiors behave.
        d. Enforcement of ethics policies is a common way of dealing with ethical problems.
        e. Codes of ethics do not need to be enforced.

____13.   Bribes are an ethical issue related to
        a. conflicts of interest.
        b. fairness and honesty.
        c. communications.
        d. business relations.
        e. marketing.

____14.   Business ethics is
        a. laws and regulations that regulate the conduct of business.
        b. standards, rules, and codes of conduct that govern the behaviour for individuals
            and groups.
        c. principles and standards that define acceptable conduct in the world of business.
        d. businesses' obligations to maximize their positive impact and minimize their
            negative impact on society.
        e. principles that describe what a person believes is the right way to behave.

____15.   Deceiving or misrepresenting the facts to customers is an ethical issue related to
        a. conflicts of interest.
        b. fairness and honesty.
        c. communications.

Chapter 3 Business Ethics and Social Responsibility

        d.   business relations.

        e.   finance.

SKILL-BUILDING QUIZ

This exercise supplements the "Build Your Skills" exercise in the textbook and is designed to help you practice your decision-making skills when you are presented with ethical dilemmas

Each of the following mini-cases poses four solutions. In some cases, only one solution is correct; in others, more than one is correct. But which is most correct? In a few mini-cases, none of the posed answers are correct. But one will be the best selection from the options listed. None of the posed answers can be changed. Pick the one that you can best justify--based on company, your experiences, your education, your ethical training, and your beliefs.

_____1.   Two of your subordinates routinely provide their children with school supplies from the office. How do you handle this situation?

      Potential Answers:

      a.   Lock up the supplies and issue them only as needed and signed for.

      b.   Tell these two subordinates that supplies are only for office use.

      c.   Report the theft of supplies to the head of security.

      d.   Send a notice to all employees that office supplies are for office use only and that disregard of this policy will result in disciplinary action.

_____2.   Your operation is being relocated. The personnel regulations are complex and might influence your employees' decisions about staying on the "team." Relocating with no experienced staff would be very difficult for you. What do you tell your employees about their options?

      Potential Answers:

      a.   State that the relocation regulations are complex. You won't go into them right now; however, "everything probably will come out OK in the end."

      b.   Suggest that they relocate with you, stating that a job in hand is worth an unknown in the bush.

      c.   Present them with your simplified version of the regulations and encourage them to "come along."

      d.   Only tell them you'd like them to relocate with you and conserve the team that has worked so well together.

_____3.   A friend of yours wants to transfer to your division, but he may not be the best qualified for the job. You do have an opening and one other person, whom you do not know, has applied. What do you do?

      Potential Answers:

      a.   Select the friend you know and in whom you have confidence.

      b.   Select the other person who you are told is qualified.

      c.   Request a qualifications comparison of the two from human resources.

      d.   Request human resources to extend the search for additional candidates before making the selection.

Chapter 3 Business Ethics and Social Responsibility

_____ 4.   Your new employee is the niece of the vice-president of finance. Her performance is
                poor, and she has caused trouble with her coworkers. What do you do?
                Potential Answers:
                a. Call her in and talk to her about her inadequacies.
                b. Ask human resources to counsel her and put her on a performance-improvement
                    plan.
                c. Go see her uncle.
                d. Since maybe it is only the "newness" of the job, give her some time to come
                    around.

Permission granted by the author of *Gray Matters: The Ethics Game,* George Sammet, Jr., Vice
President, Office of Corporate Ethics, Martin Marietta Corporation, Orlando, Florida, to use portions
of *Gray Matters: The Ethics Game* © 1992.

ANSWERS

MATCHING QUIZ

1. b   2. a   3. e   4. d   5. c

TRUE/FALSE QUIZ

1. T	5. F	9. T	13. F	17. T
2. F	6. T	10. F	14. T	18. T
3. T	7. T	11. T	15. T	19. F
4. T	8. F	12. F	16. F	20. F

MULTIPLE-CHOICE QUIZ

1. e	4. a	7. a	10. e	13. a
2. d	5. c	8. d	11. d	14. c
3. b	6. c	9. b	12. e	15. b

Chapter 3 Business Ethics and Social Responsibility

ANSWERS, POINT VALUES, AND RATIONALE FOR THE SKILL-BUILDING QUIZ

Case No.	Answer	Points	Rationale
1	A	-5	Is an example of locking everybody up; therefore, there can be no more crime. Not an efficient way to work either.
	B	10	Is directed at solving the immediate problem. But is this only the tip of an iceberg? Are there more pilferers?
	C	-5	While technically correct--is overkill.
	D	10	Is a solution aimed at the immediate problem and any continuing problem. A reiteration of company policies for comprehensive understanding.
2	A	-5	Could end up misleading your employees, as you are promising something over which you have no control.
	B	-5	Is a threat; it's the "fear" approach and does nothing to build teamwork.
	C	5	As long as your "simplified version" is not misleading.
	D	-5	Is not being fair to your employees.
3	A	-5	May not be in the best interest of the company.
	B	5	Told by whom? If by human resources, this may be a good answer.
	C	5	More clearly defines your options.
	D	10	Is favoued if you believe there may be someone out there who has even better qualifications than either your friend or the applicant.
4	A	10	As difficult as it may be for you to do, this is how the problem should be handled.
	B	5	Fails to involve you personally. It is your problem first.
	C	-5	Could solve no problem, yet might develop a new one for you.
	D	-5	Bad news never gets better with time. Guidance, counseling, training, or something else is needed.

Ferrell, Hirt, Bates & Currie, Business: A Changing World, First Edition

Chapter 4 Business in a Borderless World

Chapter 4 Business in a Borderless World

CHAPTER OBJECTIVES

After reading this chapter, you should be able to:
- Explore some of the factors within the international trade environment that influence business.
- Investigate some of the economic, legal-political, social, cultural, and technological barriers to international business.
- Specify some of the agreements, alliances, and organizations that may encourage trade across international boundaries.
- Summarize the different levels of organizational involvement in international trade.
- Contrast two basic strategies used in international business.
- Assess the opportunities and problems facing a small business considering expanding into international markets.

CHAPTER RECAP

THE ROLE OF INTERNATIONAL BUSINESS

International business refers to the buying, selling, and trading of goods and services across national boundaries. Falling political barriers and new technology are making it possible for more and more businesses to sell their products overseas as well as at home.

Nations and businesses engage in international trade to obtain raw materials and goods that would otherwise be unavailable to them. Which goods and services a nation sells depends on what resources it has. When a nation is the only source of an item, the only producer of an item, or can produce an item more efficiently than any other nation, it is said to have an **absolute advantage**. Most international trade, however, is based on **comparative advantage**, which occurs when a country specializes in products that it can supply more efficiently or at a lower cost than it can produce other items.

Exporting is the sale of goods and services to foreign markets. Importing is the purchase of goods and services from foreign sources.

A nation's **balance of trade** is the difference in value between its exports and imports. A nation that exports more than it imports has a favorable balance of trade. Because Canada exports more than it imports, it has a positive balance of trade, or **trade surplus**. The trade surplus fluctuates according to such factors as the health of the Canadian and world economy, productivity, perceived quality, and exchange rates. Canada wants to maintain a trade surplus, as it is associated with strong business, job creation and a higher standard of living. The difference between the flow of money into and out of a country is called the **balance of payments**. The balance of payments includes a country's balance of trade, foreign investments, foreign aid, military expenditures, and money spent by tourists.

Chapter 4 Business in a Borderless World

INTERNATIONAL TRADE BARRIERS

When a company decides to do business outside its own country, it will encounter a number of barriers, so it must research the other country's economic, political, legal, social, cultural, and technological backgrounds and learn how to deal with tariffs, quotas, and other concerns.

When considering doing business abroad, Canadian businesspeople cannot take for granted that other countries offer the same things as are found in *industrialized nations*--economically advanced countries such as Canada, the United States and Japan. *Less-developed countries (LDCs)* are characterized by low per capita income (income generated by the nation's production of goods and services divided by the population), which means that consumers are not as likely to purchase nonessential products. A country's level of development is determined in part by its infrastructure, the physical facilities that support economic activities, such as railroads, highways, ports, air fields, utilities and power plants, schools, hospitals, communication systems, and commercial distribution systems.

The ratio at which one nation's currency can be exchanged for another's or for gold is the **exchange rate**. A government may alter the value of its national currency. Devaluation decreases the value of a currency in relation to other currencies; it stimulates a nation's economy by encouraging other nations to buy more of the country's goods and services and discouraging its own citizens from purchasing imported items and vacationing abroad. Revaluation, which increases the value of a currency in relation to other currencies, occurs rarely.

A company that decides to enter the international marketplace must contend with potentially complex relationships among the different laws of its own nation international laws, and the laws of the nation with which it will be trading, various trade restrictions imposed on international trade, and changing political climates. Canada has a number of laws and regulations that govern the activities of Canadian firms engaged in international trade. Generally, though Canada adheres to the many agreements that have evolved from the United Nations, the World Trade Organization and other trading groups such as NAFTA, of which we are members. Outside Canadian borders, businesspeople are likely to find that the laws of other nations differ from those of Canada. Many of the legal rights that Canadians take for granted do not exist in other countries, and a firm doing business abroad must understand and obey the laws of the host country. Some countries have copyright and patent laws that are less strict than those of Canada; some countries fail to honour Canadian laws.

Tariffs and other trade restrictions are part of a country's legal structure but may be established or removed for political reasons. An **import tariff** is a tax levied by a nation on goods imported into the country. Such tariffs may be fixed (a specific amount of money levied on each unit of a product) or ad valorem (based on the value of the item). Import tariffs are commonly imposed to protect domestic products by raising the price of imported ones. Advocates of protective tariffs argue that their use protects domestic industries, particularly new ones, from well-established foreign competitors; critics counter that their use inhibits free trade and competition. **Exchange controls** restrict the amount of a particular currency that can be bought or sold. Some countries control their foreign trade by forcing businesspeople to buy and sell foreign products through a central agency such as a central bank.

A **quota** limits the number of units of a particular product that can be imported into a country. An **embargo** prohibits trade in a particular product, usually for political, economic, health, or religious

Chapter 4 Business in a Borderless World

reasons. A common reason for setting quotas is to prohibit **dumping**, which occurs when a country or business sells products at less than what it costs to produce them. Foreign businesses may engage in dumping to gain quick entry into a market, when the domestic market for a firm's product is too small to support an efficient level of production, or when technologically obsolete products are no longer salable in the country of origin.

Political considerations in international trade are seldom written down and often change rapidly. War, policies deemed unacceptable by society, and mundane political affairs affect international business daily. Businesses engaged in international trade must consider the relative instability of some nations, because a sudden change in power can result in a regime that is hostile to foreign investment. Political concerns may lead a group of companies or nations to form a **cartel**, agreeing to act as a monopoly and not compete with each other, to generate a competitive advantage in world markets.

Most businesspeople engaged in international trade underestimate the importance of social and cultural differences, which can derail an important transaction. Languages often do not translate literally, and businesses often must develop new names, packaging, and promotional material for products in foreign countries. Body language--nonverbal, usually unconscious communication through gestures, posture, and facial expression--may affect business negotiations. Some nations may have different concepts of personal space and time as well as customs and traditions that are unfamiliar to foreign businesspeople. Many countries lack the technological infrastructure found in Canada, and some marketers are viewing such barriers as opportunities. Such problems cannot always be avoided, but they can be minimized through research.

TRADE ALLIANCES, SPECIFIC MARKETS, AND TRADE SUPPORTERS

Although economic, political, legal, and sociocultural issues may seem like daunting barriers to international trade, there are also organizations and agreements that foster international trade that can help managers get involved in and succeed in global markets.

The **General Agreement on Tariffs and Trade (GATT)**, originally signed by 23 nations in 1947, provides a forum for tariff negotiations and a place where international trade problems can be discussed and resolved; it currently has more than 100 members. GATT sponsors rounds of negotiations aimed at reducing trade restrictions. The most recent round, the Uruguay Round (1988-1994), reduced trade barriers for most products and provided new rules to prevent dumping. It is hoped that reducing trade barriers will help nations develop closer relationships, and as this happens, global markets should become more efficient.

The **North American Free Trade Agreement (NAFTA)**, which went into effect on January 1, 1994, effectively merged Canada, the United States, and Mexico into one market. NAFTA eliminates most tariffs and trade restrictions on agricultural and manufactured products among the three countries over a period of 15 years. Although controversial, NAFTA has become a positive factor for Canadian firms wishing to engage in international business.

The **European Union (EU)** was established in 1958 to promote trade among its members. To facilitate free trade among its members, the EU is working toward the standardization of business regulations and requirements, import duties, and value-added taxes; the elimination of customs checks; and the creation of a standardized currency (the euro) for use by all members.

Chapter 4 Business in a Borderless World

Despite economic turmoil in recent years, companies of the Pacific Rim nations--Japan, China, South Korea, Taiwan, Singapore, Hong Kong, the Philipines, Malaysia, Indonesia, Australia, and Indochina--have become increasingly competitive and sophisticated in global business over the last three decades.

The **World Bank**, more formally known as the International Bank for Reconstruction and Development, was established and supported by the industrialized nations in 1946 to loan money to underdeveloped and developing countries. It loans its own funds or borrows funds from member nations to finance a variety or projects.

The **International Monetary Fund (IMF)** was established in 1947 to promote trade among member nations by eliminating trade barriers and fostering financial cooperation. It makes short-term loans to member countries that have balance-of-payment deficits and provides foreign currencies to member nations.

GETTING INVOLVED IN INTERNATIONAL BUSINESS

Businesses may get involved in international trade at many levels. The degree of commitment of resources and effort required increases according to the level at which a business involves itself in international trade.

Many companies first get involved in international trade when they import goods from other countries for resale in their own businesses. A business may get involved in exporting when it is called upon to supply a foreign company with a particular product. Such exporting enables firms of all sizes to participate in international business. Exporting sometimes takes place through **countertrade agreements**, which involve bartering products for other products instead of for currency. A company may market its products overseas directly or import goods directly from their manufacturer, or it may go through an export agent that handles international transactions for other firms. The advantage of using an export agent is that the company does not have to deal with foreign currencies or red tape; the disadvantage is that the business must raise its price or provide a larger discount than it would in a domestic transaction.

The next level is using a **trading company**, which buys goods in one country and sells them to buyers in another country. A trading company handles all activities required to move products from one country to another, including consulting, marketing research, advertising, insurance, product research and design, and warehousing.

Licensing is a trade arrangement in which one company--the licenser--allows another company--the licensee--to use its company name, products, patents, brands, trademarks, raw materials, and/or production processes in exchange for a royalty fee. **Franchising** is a form of licensing in which a company--the franchiser--agrees to provide a franchisee a name, logo, methods of operation, advertising, products, and other elements associated with the franchiser's business, in return for a financial commitment and the agreement to conduct business in accordance with the franchiser's standard of operations. Licensing and franchising enable a company to enter the international marketplace without spending large sums of money abroad or hiring or transferring personnel

Chapter 4 Business in a Borderless World

overseas. They also permit a business to establish goodwill for its products in a foreign land. If the licensee (or franchisee) fails to maintain high standards of quality, the product's image may be hurt.

The next level is **contract manufacturing**, which occurs when a company hires a foreign firm to produce a specified volume of the company's product to specification; the final product carries the domestic company's name.

A company that wants to do business in another country may set up a joint venture by finding a local partner (occasionally, the host nation itself) to share the costs and operation of the business. A **strategic alliance** is a partnership formed to create competitive advantage on a worldwide basis.

Direct investment is the ownership of overseas facilities. A company may control the facilities outright, or it may hold a majority ownership interest in the company that controls the facilities. **Outsourcing**, a form of direct investment, involves transferring manufacturing or other tasks to countries where labor and supplies are less expensive.

The highest level of international business involvement is the multinational corporation (**MNC**), a corporation that operates on a worldwide scale, without significant ties to any one nation or region. Multinationals often have greater assets and larger populations than some of the countries in which they do business.

INTERNATIONAL BUSINESS STRATEGIES

Planning in a global economy requires businesspeople to understand the economic legal, political, and sociocultural realities of the countries in which they will operate. These factors will affect the strategy a business chooses to use when doing business outside its own borders.

Companies doing business internationally have traditionally used a **multinational strategy**, customizing their products, promotion, and distribution according to cultural, technological, regional, and national differences. More and more companies are moving from this customization strategy to a **global strategy** (globalization), which involves standardizing products (and, as much as possible, their promotion and distribution) for the whole world, as if it were a single entity. Before moving outside their own borders, companies must conduct environmental analyses to evaluate the potential of and problems associated with various markets and to determine what strategy is best for doing business in those markets. Failure to do so may result in losses and even negative publicity.

Managers who can meet the challenges of creating and implementing effective and sensitive business strategies for the global marketplace can help lead their companies to success. Being globally aware is therefore an important quality for today's managers and will become a critical attribute for managers of the twenty-first century.

ENHANCEMENT EXERCISES

1. The Canadian government, through various departments and agencies, offers programs to encourage exports. Such services include educational assistance, guaranteed payment plans and insurance guidance to name a few. Imagine you are running a candy cane company and

Chapter 4 Business in a Borderless World

are considering exporting as a possible International business strategy. Search the Internet for federal and provincial programs that would provide assistance to you, collect the information, categorize the various programs and rate the programs according to which ones would most interest a first time candy cane exporter.

2. The federal government and several Canadian companies have been involved in trade disputes the past few years. Use the Internet, magazine articles and newspapers to trace the following disputes from start to finish. Compare the solution mechanism and the results for each.
    a) Soft wood lumber dispute with the United States
    b) Bombardier subsidy dispute

MATCHING QUIZ

Match the following key terms with the correct definition.

a. absolute advantage
b. comparative advantage
c. exchange rate
d. exchange controls
e. multinational strategy
f. global strategy

____1.   When a country specializes in products that it can supply more efficiently or at a lower cost than it can produce other items.

____2.   When companies doing business internationally customize their products, promotion, and distribution according to cultural, technological, regional, and national differences.

____3.   The ratio at which one nation's currency can be exchanged for another nation's currency or for gold.

____4.   When a country is the only source of an item, the only producer of an item, or the most efficient producer of an item.

____5.   When companies doing business internationally standardize their products (and, as much as possible, their promotion and distribution) for the whole world, as if it were a single entity.

____6.   These restrict the amount of currency that can be bought or sold.

Chapter 4 Business in a Borderless World

TRUE/FALSE QUIZ

Indicate whether each of the following statements is true or false.

_____1.   Global business is the buying, selling, and trading of goods and services across national boundaries.

_____2.   Colgate-Palmolive's development of an inexpensive, plastic, hand-powered washing machine for use in households that have no electricity illustrates the global strategy.

_____3.   The balance of trade is the difference between the flow of money into and out of a country.

_____4.   Canadian companies, competing Internationally generally adhere to laws that have evolved from NAFTA and the United Nations.

_____5.   An export agent buys goods in one country and sells them to buyers in another country.

_____6.   A nation that is the only source of an item, the only producer of an item, or can produce an item more efficiently than any other nation has an absolute advantage.

_____7.   In a contract manufacturing arrangement, the final product carries the domestic firm's name.

_____8.   Importing is the sale of goods and services to foreign markets.

_____9.   Failure to understand differences in language, customs, and traditions can derail an international business transaction.

_____10.   More than 100 nations abide by the rules of GATT.

_____11.   An ad valorem tariff is a specific amount of money levied on each unit of a product brought into a country.

_____12.   A country's level of development is determined in part by its infrastructure.

_____13.   The World Bank finances the construction of medical and educational facilities.

_____14.   Companies doing business overseas have traditionally used a multinational strategy, in which they standardize products (and, as much as possible, their promotion and distribution) for the whole world, as if it were a single entity.

_____15.   A joint venture is a partnership formed to create competitive advantage on a worldwide basis.

_____16.   Multinationals may have more assets and larger populations than the nations in which

Chapter 4 Business in a Borderless World

they do business.

_____17.   Only large corporations can participate in international business.

_____18.   A quota is the suspension of trade in a particular product by the government.

_____19.   A global strategy involves standardizing products and promotion.

_____20.   A foreign business might choose to dump its products in Canada because the domestic market for the firm's product is too small to support an efficient level of product.

MULTIPLE-CHOICE QUIZ

Choose the correct answer for each of the following questions.

_____1.   The sale of goods and services to foreign markets is
    a.   outsourcing.
    b.   international business.
    c.   global business.
    d.   exporting.
    e.   importing.

_____2.   Which of the following provides a forum where international trade problems can be discussed and resolved?
    a.   General Agreement on Tariffs and Trade
    b.   International Finance Corporation
    c.   International Monetary Fund
    d.   The North American Free Trade Agreement
    e.   World Bank

_____3.   Which of the following would enable the Canadian government to lower the cost of Canadian goods abroad and make trips to the Canada less expensive for foreign tourists?
    a.   exchange rate
    b.   exchange controls
    c.   devaluation
    d.   revaluation
    e.   unilateral price freezes

_____4.   Which of the following is a duty levied by a nation on goods bought outside its borders and imported into the country?
    a.   import tariff
    b.   fixed tariff
    c.   ad valorem tariff
    d.   protective tariff
    e.   open tariff

Chapter 4 Business in a Borderless World

_____5.	The fact that consumers the world over can drink Coca-Cola with essentially the same taste and in recognizable packaging indicates that the Coca-Cola Company is using the
	a.	monopolizing strategy.
	b.	conventional strategy.
	c.	international strategy.
	d.	multinational strategy.
	e.	global strategy.

_____6.	Which of the following involves bartering products?
	a.	outsourcing
	b.	joint venture
	c.	licensing
	d.	franchising
	e.	countertrade agreements

_____7.	A common reason for establishing quotas is to prevent which of the following?
	a.	joint ventures
	b.	countertade agreements
	c.	embargoes
	d.	dumping
	e.	cartels

_____8.	Which of the following requires the least commitment of resources and effort?
	a.	licensing
	b.	importing and exporting
	c.	direct investment
	d.	contract
	e.	multinational corporations

_____9.	A country has a comparative advantage when
	a.	it is the only source of an item.
	b.	it specializes in products that it can supply more efficiently or cheaply than it can produce other items.
	c.	it is the only producer of an item.
	d.	it is the most efficient producer of an item.
	e.	it sells products at less than what it costs to produce them.

_____10.	Which of the following is the difference in value between a nation's exports and imports?
	a.	trade deficit
	b.	balance of trade
	c.	balance of payments
	d.	exporting
	e.	exchange rate

_____11.	Which of the following makes short-term loans to member countries with trade

Chapter 4 Business in a Borderless World

deficits and provides them with foreign currencies?
a. International Monetary Fund
b. World Bank
c. International Development Association
d. International Finance Corporation
e. General Agreement on Tariffs and Trade

____12.   Which of the following is NOT an issue related to social and cultural barriers?
a. different body language
b. different language
c. different concept of time
d. different customs
e. different laws

____13.   Why is the European Union working toward the standardization of business regulations and requirements?
a. to decrease trade among its members
b. to encourage trade with non-members
c. to facilitate free trade among its members
d. to facilitate limited trade among its members
e. It has nothing to do with trade.

____14.   Companies that want more control and that have considerable resources to invest in international business will probably choose to use which of the following levels of involvement?
a. exporting
b. franchising
c. contract manufacturing
d. direct investment
e. joint venture

____15.   Which of the following is a partnership between a foreign business or government and a domestic business?
a. direct investment
b. contract manufacturing
c. joint venture
d. cartel
e. multinational corporation

Chapter 4 Business in a Borderless World

SKILL-BUILDING QUIZ

In the "Build Your Skills" exercise of Chapter 4, you "traveled the globe" by answering questions about some of the cultural norms found in other countries. Continue to build your skills by matching the country or region with the cultural descriptor provided.

a. Japan
b. Middle East
c. England
d. Latin America

_____1. To indicate a person wants two items, only the index finger is raised; holding up two fingers, as Canadians do (in a "V" shape) is considered an obscene gesture here.

_____2. The word "no" must be pronounced three times before it is accepted here.

_____3. Bowing is a traditional form of greeting here.

_____4. General arm gestures are used for emphasis here.

ANSWERS

MATCHING QUIZ

1. b   2. e   3. c   4. a   5. f   6. d

TRUE/FALSE QUIZ

1. F	5. F	9. T	13. T	17. F
2. F	6. T	10. T	14. F	18. F
3. F	7. T	11. F	15. F	19. T
4. T	8. F	12. T	16. T	20. T

MULTIPLE-CHOICE QUIZ

1. d	4. a	7. d	10. b	13. c
2. a	5. e	8. b	11. a	14. d
3. c	6. e	9. b	12. e	15. c

SKILL-BUILDING QUIZ

1. c   2. b   3. a   4. d

Chapter 5 Options for Organizing Business

CHAPTER OUTLINE

Introduction

Sole Proprietorships
      Advantages of Sole Proprietorships
      Disadvantages of Sole Proprietorships

Partnerships
      Types of Partnership
      Articles of Partnership
      Advantages of Partnerships
      Disadvantages of Partnerships
      Taxation of Partnerships

Corporations
      Creating a Corporation
      Types of Corporations
      Elements of a Corporation
      Advantages of Corporations
      Disadvantages of Corporations
      Disclosure of Information

Cooperatives

Trends in Business Ownership: Mergers and Acquisitions

CHAPTER OBJECTIVES

After reading this chapter, you should be able to:
- Define and examine the advantages and disadvantages of the sole proprietorship form of organization.
- Identify three types of partnership and evaluate the advantages and disadvantages of the partnership form of organization.
- Describe the corporate form of organization and cite the advantages and disadvantages of corporations.
- Define and debate the advantages and disadvantages of mergers, acquisitions, and leveraged buyouts.
- Propose an appropriate organizational form for a start-up business.

Chapter 5 Options for Organizing Business

CHAPTER RECAP

INTRODUCTION

A business's form of ownership affects how it operates, how much tax it pays, and how much control its owners have.

SOLE PROPRIETORSHIPS

Sole proprietorships, businesses owned and operated by one individual, are the most common form of organization in Canada. They typically are small businesses employing fewer than 50 people.

Sole proprietorships have many advantages. Because they are generally managed by their owners, they can make decisions quickly. The formation of a sole proprietorship is relatively easy and inexpensive. Sometimes, they can even operate out of a garage or spare bedroom, but more often they buy or rent space specifically for the business. Sole proprietorships permit the greatest degree of secrecy because the owners are not required to discuss operating plans with anyone. All profits from a sole proprietorship belong to the owner, who alone decides how to use them. The sole proprietor has complete control over how the business is run and can respond quickly to competitive business conditions or to changes in the economy. Sole proprietorships also have the most freedom from government regulation. Profits from the business are considered personal income and are taxed at individual tax rates, which are lower than corporate tax rates for large companies. Finally, the sole proprietorship is easily dissolved as long as all debts have been paid.

Sole proprietorships have several disadvantages, but these depend on the goals and talents of the individual owner. The sole proprietor has unlimited liability in meeting the debts of the business and may have to use personal, nonbusiness holdings to pay off the venture's debts. Among the relatively few sources of money available to the sole proprietor are a bank, friends, family, the Small Business Administration, or his or her own funds. A sole proprietorship's credit standing reflects the owner's personal financial condition, and the owner may have to use personal assets to guarantee loans. The sole proprietor must be a generalist, performing many functions, including management, marketing, finance, accounting, bookkeeping, and personnel. The life expectancy of a sole proprietorship is directly related to that of the owner and his or her ability to work. It may be difficult to sell a proprietorship and at the same time assure customers that the business will continue to meet their needs. Because it is difficult for sole proprietorships to match the wages and benefits offered by large corporations and there is little room for advancement, they may have difficulty attracting and retaining qualified employees. Taxes may be an advantage or disadvantage depending on the sole proprietorship's income.

PARTNERSHIPS

Partnerships are associations of two or more persons who carry on as co-owners of a business for profit.

A **general partnership** involves a complete sharing in the management of a business; each partner has unlimited liability for the debts of the business. A **limited partnership** has at least one general partner who assumes unlimited liability and management responsibility, and at least one limited partner whose liability is limited to his or her investment and who does not participate in the firm's management. A

Chapter 5 Options for Organizing Business

joint venture is a partnership of individuals and/or organizations established for a specific project or for a limited time.

Most states require **articles of partnership**, legal documents that set forth the basic agreement between the partners. Articles of partnership usually list the partnership capital (money or assets that each partner has contributed to the partnership), state each partner's individual role or duty, specify how the profits and losses of the partnership will be divided among the partners, and describe how a partner may leave the partnership and any other restrictions that might apply to the agreement.

Starting a partnership is easy, usually requiring little more than drawing up the articles of partnership. When a business has several partners, it benefits from the combination of talents and skills and pooled financial resources. Partnerships tend to be larger than sole proprietorships and, thus, have greater earning power and better credit ratings. They can provide diverse skills because partners can specialize in their areas of expertise. Small partnerships can react more quickly to changes in the business environment than can large partnerships and corporations. Partnerships have fewer regulatory controls affecting their financial activities than do public corporations and do not generally have to file public financial statements with government agencies.

Partnerships also have several disadvantages. Limited partners have no voice in the management of the business and may bear most of the risk. A clash in organizational cultures or a change in the goals of one partner may cause conflict. General partners have unlimited liability for the firm's debts, a real disadvantage when one partner has greater financial resources than the others. All partners are responsible for the business actions of the other partners. A partnership is terminated when a partner dies or withdraws; other partners who wish to continue the business face a disruption in business and a loss of finances and management skills. Selling a partnership interest is difficult because it is hard to assess the value of a partner's share. Partners share the profits in accordance with the articles of partnership which may be a disadvantage if the division of the profits does not reflect the work each partner puts into the venture. Partnerships have limited sources of funds because the business has no public value.

Partnerships are quasi-taxable organizations, meaning that they do not pay taxes when submitting the partnership's tax return to the Internal Revenue Service instead, the partners must pay individual taxes on their share of the profits. The tax return provides information about the organization's profitability and the distribution of profits among the partners.

CORPORATIONS

A **corporation** is a legal entity, created by the provincial or federal government, whose assets and liabilities are separate from its owners'. As a legal entity, a corporation can receive, own, and transfer property, enter into contracts with individuals or other corporations, and sue (or be sued) in court. The owners of a corporation own shares of the firm, called stock, which can be traded. The stockholders, or shareholders, are entitled to all profits that are left after all the corporation's other obligations have been paid. These profits are distributed in the form of cash payments called **dividends**.

A corporation is created under the laws of the government in which it incorporates. A corporation's name cannot be similar to that of another business. The incorporators must file articles of incorporation with the appropriate government office containing basic information about the firm, such as: (1) name and address, (2) corporate objectives, (3) classes of stock and the number of shares

Chapter 5 Options for Organizing Business

for each class issued, (4) expected life of the corporation (usually forever), (5) financial capital required at the time of incorporation, (6) provisions for transferring shares of stock between owners, (7) provisions for the regulation of internal corporate affairs, (8) address of the business office registered with the state of incorporation, (9) names and addresses of the initial board of directors, and (10) names and addresses of the incorporators. Based on this information, the government issues a **corporate charter** to the company.

A **private corporation** is owned by just one or a few people who are closely involved in managing the business; its stock is not traded publicly. A **public corporation** is one whose stock anyone may buy, sell, or trade. A private corporation may "go public" by selling stock to the public; a public corporation may be "taken private" when one or a few individuals purchase all the firm's stock so that it can no longer be sold publicly. A **subsidiary corporation** is one that has the majority of its stock owned by another corporation known as the parent company. The subsidiary company has its own corporate structure with a president and other senior officers. A **holding company** is a special type of corporation that controls one or more other corporations through ownership of their common stock. **Crown corporations** are owned and operated by a federal, provincial, or local government and provide a service to citizens, such as mail delivery, and earn a profit. **Nonprofit corporations** focus on providing a service rather than earning a profit, but they are not owned by a government entity.

A **board of directors**, elected by the shareholders to oversee the general operation of the corporation, sets the long-range objectives of the corporation. The board is responsible for ensuring that the objectives are achieved on schedule and is legally liable for the mismanagement of the firm or for any misappropriation of funds. The board of directors hires corporate officers who are responsible to the directors for the management and daily operations of the firm. Directors may be employees and officers of the company (inside directors) or people unaffiliated with the company (outside directors).

There are two basic types of corporate ownership. Owners of **preferred stock** are a special class of owners because, although they generally do not have any say in running the company, they have a claim to any profits before any other stockholders do. Most preferred stock carries a cumulative claim to dividends, which means that if the company does not pay preferred-stock dividends in one year because of losses, the dividends accumulate to the next year. Although owners of **common stock** do not get such preferential treatment with regard to dividends, they do get some say in the operation of the corporation. Their ownership gives them the right to vote for members of the board of directors and on other important issues. Common shareholders may vote by *proxy,* which is a written authorization by which shareholders assign their voting privilege to someone else, who then votes for his or her choice at the shareholders' meeting. In most states, when the corporation decides to sell new shares of common stock in the marketplace, common shareholders have a *preemptive right* to purchase new shares of the stock from the corporation.

Corporations have some specific advantages over other forms of business ownership. Because the corporation's assets (money and resources) and liabilities (debts and other obligations) are separate from its owners', in most cases the shareholders are not held responsible for the firm's debts if it fails or is sued. Shareholders can transfer shares of stock to others without affecting the corporation, and they can do so without prior approval of other shareholders. A corporation is usually chartered to last forever unless its articles of incorporation state otherwise. Public corporations can raise long-term funds more easily than other forms of business because their stocks and bonds (debt securities) are traded in public markets. Because long-term financing is readily available, large corporations can easily expand into national and international markets.

Chapter 5 Options for Organizing Business

The corporate form of organization also has several disadvantages. Corporations pay taxes on their income and, if profits are distributed in the form of dividends, the dividends are taxed a second time as part of the shareholders' income. If a holding company is involved, triple taxation may occur. The formation of a corporation can be costly. Corporations must make information available to their owners, usually in an annual report, which contains financial information and describes the company's operations, plans, and products. Public corporations must also file reports with the Securities and Exchange Commission (SEC), a government regulatory agency. Finally, the employees of a corporation are generally not shareholders and, consequently, they may feel that their work benefits only the shareholders and fail to see how they fit into the corporate picture.

COOPERATIVES

A **cooperative (co-op)** is an organization composed of individuals or small businesses that have banded together to reap the benefits of belonging to a larger organization. A co-op is not intended to earn a profit, but rather to make its members more profitable or save money. A co-op can purchase supplies in large quantities and pass the savings on to its members. It can also help advertise and distribute its members' products more efficiently than each member could on an individual basis.

TRENDS IN BUSINESS OWNERSHIP: MERGERS AND ACQUISITIONS

Companies large and small achieve growth and improve profitability by expanding their operations, often by developing and selling new products or selling current products to new groups of customers in different geographic areas, and by merging with or purchasing other companies. A **merger** occurs when two companies (usually corporations) combine to form a new company. An **acquisition** occurs when one company purchases another by buying most of its stock. Mergers may be horizontal (between firms that make and sell similar products to the same customer), vertical (between firms that operate at different but related levels in an industry), or conglomerate (between firms in unrelated businesses). When a company (or a corporate raider) wants to acquire another company, it offers to buy some or all of the other company's stock at a premium over its current price in a friendly or hostile tender offer. To head off a hostile takeover attempt, a threatened company's managers may ask shareholders not to sell to the raider; file a lawsuit in an effort to abort the takeover; initiate a poison pill (whereby the firm allows shareholders to buy more shares of stock at prices lower than the current market value) or shark repellent (whereby management requires a large majority of shareholders to approve the takeover); seek a white knight (a more acceptable firm that is willing to acquire the threatened company); or take the company private. In a **leveraged buyout (LBO)**, a group of investors borrows money from banks and other institutions to acquire a company (or a division of one), using the assets of the purchased company to guarantee repayment of the loan.

Some people view mergers and acquisitions favorably because they enable companies to gain a larger market share in their industries, to enhance their ability to compete, to acquire valuable assets such as new products or plants and equipment, to lower their costs, to boost their stock prices, and sometimes to make a quick profit. Critics argue that mergers hurt companies because they force managers to focus their efforts on avoiding takeovers rather than managing their companies effectively and profitably; sometimes force companies to take on a heavy debt burden to stave off a takeover; and damage employee morale and productivity, as well as the quality of the companies' products.

Chapter 5 Options for Organizing Business

ENHANCEMENT EXERCISE

Investigate what type of business ownership is preferable and why. Interview business owners on the various types of ownership. If you were to start a business, what form would it take?

MATCHING QUIZ

Match each of the following statements with the correct key term.

a. private corporation
b. public corporation
c. subsidiary corporation
d. holding company
e. Crown corporations
f. nonprofit corporations

_____1. An organization that controls one or more other corporations through ownership of their common stock.

_____2. An organization owned by one or a few people who are closely involved in managing the business.

_____3. An organization whose stock anyone may buy or sell or trade.

_____4. An organization owned and operated by a federal, provincial, or local government.

_____5. An organization that has the majority of its stock owned by another corporation known as the parent company.

_____6. An organization that focuses on providing a service rather than earning a profit, but is not owned by a government.

Chapter 5 Options for Organizing Business

TRUE/FALSE QUIZ

Indicate whether each of the following statements is true or false.

_____1.   A limited partnership involves complete sharing in the management of the business.

_____2.   A board of directors is liable for the mismanagement of the organization.

_____3.   Shareholders are personally liable for the debts of a corporation in which they hold stock.

_____4.   A limited liability company is an organization of small businesses that have banded together to reap the benefits of belonging to a larger organization.

_____5.   Corporations are usually set up to last forever.

_____6.   A merger occurs when one company purchases another.

_____7.   The stock of private corporations is traded on the open market.

_____8.   A conglomerate merger results when two firms in unrelated industries merge.

_____9.   Sole proprietorships allow the greatest degree of secrecy of all the organizational forms.

_____10.   Partnerships tend to have better credit ratings than sole proprietorships.

_____11.   Common shareholders receive dividend payments before preferred stockholders.

_____12.   Corporate income may be taxed twice or even three times.

_____13.   There are no restrictions on the number of shareholders allowed in a corporation.

_____14.   Partnerships do not pay taxes on their income.

_____15.   The sole proprietorship form of organization permits the greatest degree of control.

_____16.   A subsidiary corporation is one that has control over one or more other corporations through ownership of its common stock.

_____17.   Sole proprietorships can attract and retain employees easier than can corporations.

_____18.   A foreign corporation is one doing business in another nation.

_____19.   Selling a partnership interest may be problematic because it has no public value.

_____20.   Mergers can help boost a company's value but may do so at the expense of its productivity and employee morale.

Chapter 5 Options for Organizing Business

MULTIPLE-CHOICE QUIZ

Choose the correct answer for each of the following questions.

_____1. Which of the following is an advantage of partnerships?
   a. unlimited liability
   b. business responsibility
   c. limited source of funds
   d. responsibility of partners for other partners' actions
   e. specialization

_____2. Which of the following forms of organization is most common in Canada?
   a. holding company
   b. corporation
   c. partnership
   d. sole proprietorship
   e. cooperative

_____3. Which of the following is NOT in an article of partnership?
   a. statement of money/assets contributed by each partner
   b. statement of each partner's management role
   c. statement of classes and number of stocks issued
   d. statement of how profits and losses are distributed
   e. provisions for leaving the partnership

_____4. Which of the following is a disadvantage of sole proprietorships?
   a. ease and cost of formation
   b. limited source of funds
   c. control of the business
   d. secrecy
   e. single taxation

_____5. Which of the following has all of its stock owned by a few people and none of its shares sold to the public?
   a. public corporation
   b. subsidiary corporation
   c. private corporation
   d. cooperative
   e. sole proprietorship

_____6. Which of the following has the majority of its stock owned by another corporation?
   a. subsidiary corporation
   b. holding company
   c. cooperative
   d. limited partnership
   e. joint venture

Chapter 5 Options for Organizing Business

_____7.	Which of the following is a disadvantage of the corporate form of organization?
   a.	limited liability of shareholders
   b.	perpetual life
   c.	sources of capital
   d.	double taxation
   e.	expansion potential

_____8.	Which of the following is an advantage of sole proprietorships?
   a.	secrecy
   b.	expansion potential
   c.	limited sources of funds
   d.	unlimited liability
   e.	specialization

_____9.	Which of the following may result in triple taxation?
   a.	subsidiary corporation
   b.	holding company
   c.	cooperative
   d.	sole proprietorship
   e.	general partnership

_____10.	Which of the following is set up for a specific project or for a limited time?
   a.	joint venture
   b.	sole proprietorship
   c.	general partnership
   d.	limited partnership
   e.	subsidiary corporation

_____11.	Which of the following represents a bid to buy some or all of another company's stock at a premium over its current price?
   a.	white knight
   b.	poison pill
   c.	leveraged buyout
   d.	merger mania
   e.	tender offer

_____12.	Which of the following company?
   a.	improved employee morale
   b.	reduced debt
   c.	lowered stock price
   d.	enhanced ability to compete
   e.	increased costs

Chapter 5 Options for Organizing Business

_____13.   Which of the following is a disadvantage of partnerships?
   a. perpetual life
   b. double taxation
   c. unlimited liability
   d. expansion potential
   e. ability to specialize

_____14.   Which of the following allows a shareholder to assign his or her voting rights to someone else?
   a. preemptive right
   b. proxy
   c. corporate charter
   d. Securities and Exchange Commission
   e. management

_____15.   Which of the following pays taxes on its income?
   a. sole proprietorship
   b. general partnership
   c. limited partnership
   d. joint venture
   e. public corporation

SKILL-BUILDING QUIZ

In the "Build Your Skills" exercise of your text, you were asked to focus on the advantages and disadvantages of each of the forms of business ownership. Build on those skills by choosing the correct answer for each of the following questions.

_____1.   Which of the following forms of organization offers its owners the greatest secrecy and degree of control over the operations of the business?
   a. public corporation
   b. limited partnership
   c. sole proprietorship
   d. private corporation
   e. cooperative

_____2.   Which of the following forms of organization has the greatest access to funds?
   a. public corporation
   b. partnership
   c. sole proprietorship
   d. private corporation
   e. cooperative

Chapter 5 Options for Organizing Business

_____3.   Which of the following forms of organization may cause problems if one owner makes
            a bad decision that puts the other owners' personal resources in jeopardy?
            a.   public corporation
            b.   partnership
            c.   sole proprietorship
            d.   private corporation
            e.   cooperative

_____4.   Which of the following forms of organization does not earn a profit?
            a.   public corporation
            b.   partnership
            c.   sole proprietorship
            d.   private corporation
            e.   cooperative

ANSWERS

MATCHING QUIZ

1. d   2. a   3. b   4. e   5. c   6. f

TRUE/FALSE QUIZ

1. F	5. T	9. T	13. F	17. F
2. T	6. F	10. T	14. T	18. F
3. F	7. F	11. F	15. T	19. T
4. F	8. T	12. T	16. F	20. T

MULTIPLE-CHOICE QUIZ

1. e	4. b	7. d	10. a	13. c
2. d	5. c	8. a	11. e	14. b
3. c	6. a	9. b	12. d	15. e

SKILL-BUILDING QUIZ

1. c   2. a   3. b   4. e

Chapter 6 Small Business, Entrepreneurship, and Franchising

CHAPTER OUTLINE

Introduction

The Nature of Entrepreneurship and Small Business
        What Is a Small Business?
        The Role of Small Business in the Canadian Economy
        Industries that Attract Small Business

Advantages of Small-Business Ownership
        Personal Advantages
        Business Advantages

Disadvantages of Small-Business Ownership
        High Stress Level
        High Failure Rate

Starting a Small Business
        The Business
        Forms of Business Ownership
        Financial Resources
        Approaches to Starting a Small Business
        Help for Small-Business Managers

Making Big Businesses Act "Small"

CHAPTER OBJECTIVES

After reading this chapter, you should be able to:
- Define entrepreneurship and small business.
- Investigate the importance of small business in the Canadian economy and why certain fields attract small business.
- Specify the advantages of small-business ownership.
- Summarize the disadvantages of small-business ownership and analyze why many small businesses fail.
- Describe how you go about starting a small business and what resources are needed.
- Explain why many large businesses are trying to "think small."
- Assess two entrepreneurs' plans for starting a small business.

CHAPTER RECAP

INTRODUCTION

There are approximately 2 million small businesses operating in Canada today, each representing the vision of their entrepreneurial owners to succeed by providing new or better products.

Chapter 6 Small Business, Entrepreneurship, and Franchising

THE NATURE OF ENTREPRENEURSHIP AND SMALL BUSINESS

An entrepreneur is a person who risks his or her wealth, time, and effort to develop for profit an innovative product or way of doing something. **Entrepreneurship** is the process of creating and managing a business to achieve desired objectives. Pushed by technological advances and alliances with other businesses, the entrepreneurship movement is accelerating with many new, smaller businesses emerging.

Defining a small business is difficult because smallness is relative. Your text defines a **small business** as any independently owned and operated business that is not dominant in its competitive area and does not employ more than 500 people. This definition is similar to the one used by the Federal Export Development Program, that defines small business as having less than $10,000,000 in annual sales and fewer than 100 employees.

Small businesses are the heart of the Canadian economy. Over 99 percent of all Canadian firms are classified as small. These small businesses are largely responsible for fueling job creation and innovation. In recent years, 85% of the 2.5 million new jobs in the private sector were created by new companies. Many small businesses today are being started because of encouragement from larger ones. Small businesses are also important because they contribute innovation, which further fuels the economy.

Small businesses are found in virtually every industry, but retailing and wholesaling, services, manufacturing, and high technology are especially attractive to entrepreneurs because they are relatively easy to enter and require low initial financing. Small-business owners also find it easier to focus on a specific group of consumers in these fields than in others, and new firms in these industries suffer less from heavy competition, at least in the early stages, than do established firms. Retailing--acquiring goods from producers or wholesalers and selling them to consumers--attracts entrepreneurs because gaining experience and exposure in retailing is easy, and it does not require a large financial investment in equipment and distribution systems. Wholesalers supply products to industrial, retail, and institutional users for resale or for use in making other products. Services, which include businesses that work for others but do not actually produce tangible goods, dominated employment growth in 2000 with 90% of new jobs created coming from this segment of the Canadian economy. Manufacturing goods can provide unique opportunities for small businesses because they can often customize products to meet specific customer needs and wants. High technology is a broad term for businesses that depend on advanced scientific and engineering knowledge.

ADVANTAGES OF SMALL-BUSINESS OWNERSHIP

Establishing and running a small business brings many personal and business advantages. Independence and freedom are major personal reasons why entrepreneurs go into business for themselves. Some small-business owners simply cannot work for someone else or want the freedom to choose with whom they work, the flexibility to pick where and when to work, and the option of working in a family setting: Additionally, small businesses often require less money to start and maintain than do large ones. With small size comes the flexibility to adapt to changing market demands and to make decisions quickly. Small firms can focus their efforts on a few key customers or on a precisely defined group of customers. They can also develop enviable reputations for quality and service.

Chapter 6 Small Business, Entrepreneurship, and Franchising

DISADVANTAGES OF SMALL-BUSINESS OWNERSHIP

Small-business owners face both psychological and physical stresses because they must work long hours and function as owner, manager, sales force, shipping and receiving clerk, bookkeeper, and custodian. There are always worries about competition, employee problems, new equipment, expanding inventory, rent increases, or changing market demand.

There is no guarantee that a small business will succeed. Small businesses fail for many reasons: a poor business concept, the burdens imposed by government regulation insufficient funds to withstand slow sales, and vulnerability to competition from larger companies. The most common causes of small-business failure include undercapitalization--the lack of funds to operate a business normally--as well as management inexperience and incompetence and inability to cope with growth.

STARTING A SMALL BUSINESS

To start any business, large or small, you must first have an idea. Next, you need to devise a **business plan**--a precise statement of the rationale for the business and a step-by-step explanation of how it will achieve its goals--to guide planning and development in the business. The business plan should include an explanation of the business, an analysis of the competition, estimates of income and expenses, a strategy for acquiring sufficient funds to keep the business going, and other information.

After developing a business plan, the entrepreneur has to decide on an appropriate legal form of business ownership whether to operate as a sole proprietorship, partnership, or corporation.

The entrepreneur must also provide or obtain money (capital) to start the business and to keep it running smoothly. The most important source of funds for any new business is the owner, who may be able to provide capital in the form of savings or borrow against the value of his or her home or some types of savings. Additionally, the owner may bring to the business personal assets such as a computer or car. Such financing is referred to as equity financing because the owner uses real personal assets instead of borrowing funds from outside sources to get started in a new business. Small businesses can also obtain equity financing by finding investors. They may sell stock in the business to family members, friends, employees, or **venture capitalists**--persons or organizations that agree to provide some funds for a new business in exchange for an ownership interest or stock.

New businesses sometimes borrow over half of their financial resources. They can also look to family and friends for loans (often at favourable rates) or other assets. The amount a bank or other institution is willing to loan depends on its assessment of the venture's likelihood of success and of the entrepreneur's ability to repay the loan. A bank will often require the business owner to put up collateral, a financial interest in the property or fixtures of the business, to guarantee payment of the debt. Additionally, the small-business owner may have to offer some personal property as collateral, such as the owner's home, in which case the loan is called a mortgage. Banks and other financial institutions can also grant a line of credit--an agreement by which a financial institution promises to lend the business a predetermined sum on demand. Small businesses may obtain funding from their suppliers in the form of trade credit--that is, suppliers allow the business to take possession of the needed goods and services and pay for them at a later date or in installments. Occasionally, small businesses engage in bartering. The federal and provincial Governments provide numerous programs to foster new business growth. These programs often take the form of loan guarantees. One such

Chapter 6 Small Business, Entrepreneurship, and Franchising

program is established under the Canadian Small Business Financing Program delivered through a network of community groups called Community Business Development Corporations.

Although entrepreneurs often start new small businesses from scratch, they may elect instead to buy an already existing business. Many small-business owners find entry into the business world through franchising. A license to sell another's products or to use another's name in business, or both, is a **franchise**. The company that sells the franchise is the **franchiser**; the purchaser of a franchise is a **franchisee**. The franchisee acquires the rights to a name, logo, methods of operation, national advertising, products, and other elements associated with the franchiser's business in return for a financial commitment and the agreement to conduct business in accordance with the franchiser's standard of operations. The franchisee pays the franchiser a monthly or annual fee based on a percentage of sales or profits. In return, the franchisee often receives building specifications and designs, site recommendations, management and accounting support and, perhaps most importantly, immediate name recognition.

Because of the crucial role that small business and entrepreneurs play in the Canadian economy, numerous organizations offer programs to improve the small-business owner's ability to compete. Entrepreneurs can learn critical marketing, management, and finance skills in seminars and college courses. Local and national publications can also provide advice. The federal government provides a wealth of information and guidance for small business though its web sites; Strategis, Business Gateway and Canadian Business Service Centres. The Small Business Administration offers many types of management assistance to small businesses, including counseling for firms in difficulty, consulting on improving operations, and training for owner/managers and their employees. The SBA also funds Small-Business Development Centers (SBDCs)--business clinics that provide counseling at no charge and training at only a nominal charge.

MAKING BIG BUSINESSES ACT "SMALL"

More and more large companies are emulating small businesses in an effort to improve their own competitiveness, flexibility, and productivity. Beginning in the 1980s and continuing through the present, large companies have been *downsizing* reducing management layers, corporate staff, and work tasks to become more flexible, resourceful, and innovative like a smaller business. Other firms have sought to make their businesses "smaller" by making their operating units function more like independent small businesses, each responsible for its profits, losses, and resources. Trying to capitalize on small-business success in introducing innovative new products, more and more companies are trying to instill a spirit of entrepreneurship into even the largest firms. In large firms, **intrapreneurs**, like entrepreneurs, take responsibility for, or "champion," developing innovations of any kind *within* the larger organization.

Chapter 6 Small Business, Entrepreneurship, and Franchising

ENHANCEMENT EXCERCISES

1. As discussed in the chapter, franchising was listed as one of the most popular methods of becoming a small business owner. Select three to five franchises you are interested in and investigate the background, various requirements, agreements and rights associated with the company. Prepare a written report that includes a summary of this information and a discussion of which franchise offers the best opportunity for investment. Take the process a step further and contact a local or national franchisee with a list of prepared questions. Make sure you ask the most important question of all: "Given the chance, would you invest in the franchise again?"

MATCHING QUIZ

Match the following statements with the correct key term.

a. entrepreneurship
b. franchise
c. franchiser
d. franchisee
e. intrapreneurs

_____1.   A company that sells a franchise.

_____2.   The process of creating and managing a business to achieve desired objectives.

_____3.   A purchaser of a franchise.

_____4.   A license to sell another's products or to use another's name in business, or both.

_____5.   In large firms, they "champion" developing innovations of any kind within the larger organization.

TRUE/FALSE QUIZ

Indicate whether each of the following statements is true or false.

_____1.   A small business is any firm that employs fewer than 1,500 people.

_____2.   New businesses sometimes borrow over half of their financing needs.

_____3.   Franchising began in the United States when Singer used it to sell sewing machines in the nineteenth century.

_____4.   A business plan should act as a guide, not limit the business's flexibility and decision making.

Chapter 6 Small Business, Entrepreneurship, and Franchising

____5.   Entrepreneurs are individuals who take responsibility for, or "champion," the development of innovations within a larger organization.

____6.   Small businesses can focus their efforts on a few key customers or a precisely defined market niche.

____7.   Exporting by small businesses is prohibited.

____8.   Small businesses must operate as sole proprietorships.

____9.   Companies with fewer than 20 employees have created most of all new jobs in recent years.

____10.   The shortest path to business failure is undercapitalization.

____11.   Small businesses employing fewer than 20 people account for just 0.1 percent of all businesses.

____12.   One of the most significant strengths of small businesses is their ability to innovate and bring significant changes and benefits to customers.

____13.   Retailing, services, manufacturing, and high technology are especially attractive fields for prospective small-business owners.

____14.   Downsizing involves increasing management layers, corporate staff, and work tasks in order to make the firm more like a small business.

____15.   A franchiser is one who purchases a franchise.

____16.   ACE, the Association of Collegiate Entrepreneurs promote entrepreneurship on university campuses throughout Canada.

____17.   Small businesses are not important to the Canadian economy.

____18.   A mortgage is any property used to secure a debt.

____19.   Independence is one of the leading reasons that entrepreneurs choose to go into business for themselves.

____20.   Small-business owners work short hours and take frequent vacations.

Chapter 6 Small Business, Entrepreneurship, and Franchising

MULTIPLE-CHOICE QUIZ

Choose the correct answer for each of the following questions.

_____1.   Which of the following is NOT a disadvantage of small-business ownership?
   a.   business failure
   b.   financial loss
   c.   psychological stress
   d.   absolute control over business decisions
   e.   physical stress

_____2.   Which of the following industries are especially attractive to entrepreneurs?
   a.   retailing and wholesaling
   b.   services
   c.   manufacturing
   d.   high technology
   e.   all of the above

_____3.   Which of the following is a program administrated by the federal government that offers loan guarantees to small businesses?
   a.   Small Business Administration
   b.   Federal Export Loan Program
   c.   Minority Enterprise Small Business Investment Companies
   d.   Association of Collegiate Entrepreneurs
   e.   Canada Small Business Financing Program

_____4.   Which of the following takes responsibility for, or "champions," the development of innovations within a larger organization?
   a.   Small Business Administration
   b.   franchisers
   c.   venture capitalists
   d.   entrepreneurs
   e.   intrapreneurs

_____5.   Which of the following may be a disadvantage of small-business ownership?
   a.   flexibility to adapt to changing markets
   b.   ability to focus on precisely defined market niches
   c.   lack of management skills to cope with growth
   d.   rapid decision making
   e.   development of reputation for quality and service

_____6.   Which of the following is NOT a business advantage of small-business ownership?
   a.   lower initial starting costs
   b.   independence
   c.   flexibility
   d.   ability to focus on a specific niche
   e.   ability to develop a good reputation

Ferrell, Hirt, Bates & Currie, Business: A Changing World, First Edition

Chapter 6 Small Business, Entrepreneurship, and Franchising

_____7. Which of the following is a business advantage to establishing and running a small business?
- a. independence
- b. high costs
- c. flexibility
- d. choice of whom to work with
- e. high technology

_____8. Which of the following may agree to provide some funds for a new business in exchange for an ownership interest, or stock?
- a. Small Business Administration
- b. financial institutions
- c. entrepreneurs
- d. intrapreneurs
- e. venture capitalists

_____9. According to your text, which of the following should be considered a small business?
- a. a firm that does not employ more than 2,500 people
- b. a firm that does not employ more than 500 people
- c. a firm with a local orientation
- d. a firm with a small market share compared to the industry as a whole
- e. an independently owned and operated firm that is not dominant in its competitive area and does not employ more than 500 people

_____10. Which of the following is a reason why so many entrepreneurs start retailing businesses?
- a. low initial financing costs
- b. heavy competition from established businesses
- c. high expenditures in distribution systems required
- d. difficulty in establishing a market niche
- e. difficulty in gaining exposure

_____11. Which of the following are business clinics held on college campuses that provide counseling and training for small-business owners?
- a. Small-Business Development Centers
- b. MESBICs
- c. Small Business Institutes
- d. Service Corps of Retired Executives
- e. university business courses

_____12. Which of the following was the fastest-growing sector of the Canadian economy in the year 2000?
- a. retailing
- b. wholesaling
- c. manufacturing
- d. services
- e. high technology

Chapter 6 Small Business, Entrepreneurship, and Franchising

_____13.   Which of the following is NOT a reason for starting a small business?
    a.   want to be own boss
    b.   want job security and fringe benefits
    c.   cannot work for other people
    d.   want to choose where and when to work
    e.   want to work at home near family

_____14.   Which of the following is a license to sell another's products or to use another's name, or both?
    a.   small business
    b.   franchiser
    c.   franchisee
    d.   franchise
    e.   business plan

_____15.   Which of the following is NOT a reason for business failure?
    a.   poor business concept
    b.   government regulation
    c.   reputation
    d.   undercapitalization
    e.   vulnerability to competition from larger companies

SKILL-BUILDING QUIZ

After reading about the successful (and not so successful) entrepreneurs in this chapter, you may be wondering if you have what it takes to be a successful entrepreneur. Beyond the creativity skills you worked on in the "Build Your Skills" exercise of your text, research has identified 25 characteristics of successful entrepreneurs.[1] These 25 characteristics provide the basis for the self-assessment below.

To assess your entrepreneurial flair, after reading column two, "Ways to Exhibit This Characteristic," check the appropriate box to indicate whether that trait describes you "almost never," "sometimes," "usually," or "almost always." Then complete the scoring section at the end of the chart. When done, read the "Indications from Scoring" chart at the end of this chapter.

1. J. A. Homady, "Research about Living Entrepreneurs," in C. A. Kent, D. L. Sexton, and K. H. Vesper Encyclopedia for Entrepreneurship (Englewood Cliffs, NJ.: Prentice Hall, Inc., 1982).

Chapter 6 Small Business, Entrepreneurship, and Franchising

Characteristic	Ways to Exhibit This Characteristic	This Describes Me			
		Almost Never	Sometimes	Usually	Almost Always
Ability to get along with people	• Considerate of and sensitive to others' needs and feelings • Understand what makes people tick • Maintain control when dealing with difficult people and situations				
Ability to take calculated risks	• Develop a well-thought-out "game plan" that will move resources toward accomplishment of goals				
Creativity	• Imaginative • Think "outside the box" to find innovative solutions to problems				
Determination	• Persistent in pursuing your goals				
Diligence	• Work to complete objectives, avoiding procrastination • Take the initiative to do what needs to be done without having to be told				
Dynamism	• Forceful and vigorous • Make choices and take action that leads to change				
Energy	• Vital and intense in your pursuits • Willing to work long and hard hours				

Chapter 6 Small Business, Entrepreneurship, and Franchising

Characteristic	Ways to Exhibit This Characteristic	This Describes Me			
		Almost Never	Sometimes	Usually	Almost Always
Flexibility	• Adapt to changing circumstances • Like being able to choose where and when to work				
Foresight	• Look and plan ahead • Know where you're going • Have concern for the future				
Independence	• Willing to stand alone • Not overly influenced by opinions of others				
Initiative	• Face and deal with difficulties and problems rather than withdrawing from or avoiding them • Productive				
Knowledge of the market	• Work to comprehend the economics of the industry you're in or hope to get into • Exercise good judgment in decisions and actions • Reason deductively and inductively				
Knowledge of product and technology	• Develop technical expertise beyond your formal education • Think strategically • Reason analytically				

Ferrell, Hirt, Bates & Currie, Business: A Changing World, First Edition

Chapter 6 Small Business, Entrepreneurship, and Franchising

Characteristic	Ways to Exhibit This Characteristic	This Describes Me			
		Almost Never	Sometimes	Usually	Almost Always
Leadership	• Exemplify a strong desire to lead • Willing to accept responsibility • Desire to influence others				
Need to achieve	• Desire to get ahead • Work long hours with high energy and enthusiasm				
Optimism	• Motivate others by your attitude and by what you say and do • Positive about the future • Dynamic, uplifting, enthusiastic				
Perceptiveness	• Initiative • Able to get to the "bottom line" in complex situations				
Perseverance	• Always working to accomplish goals in many areas of your life • Possess a "stick-to-it-iveness" in pursuing important goals				
Positive responses to challenges	• Choose to emphasize the positives, even in negative situations • See problems as opportunities				

Chapter 6 Small Business, Entrepreneurship, and Franchising

Characteristic	Ways to Exhibit This Characteristic	This Describes Me			
		Almost Never	Sometimes	Usually	Almost Always
Profit orientation	• Take actions that are best for the organization, even if those actions are unpopular with employees				
Resourcefulness	• Capable of acting effectively in difficult situations • Find a way to get something done when others believe it can't be done				
Responsiveness to criticism	• Appreciate and utilize opinions that differ from your own				
Responsiveness to suggestions	• Seek counsel from others before making decisions • Respect others' ideas				
Self-confidence	• Believe in your ability to get the job done • Remain calm and confident in times of crisis • Gain the trust of others by being sure of your own actions • Be assertive and decisive				
Versatility	• Capability of doing many things competently				
Total checks in each column					
Multiply by		X1	X2	X3	X4
Total in each column					
GRAND TOTAL POINTS (add total points from all four columns)					

Ferrell, Hirt, Bates & Currie, Business: A Changing World, First Edition

Chapter 6 Small Business, Entrepreneurship, and Franchising

ANSWERS

MATCHING QUIZ

1. c   2. a   3. d   4. b   5. e

TRUE/FALSE QUIZ

1. F	5. F	9. T	13. T	17. F
2. T	6. T	10. T	14. F	18. F
3. T	7. F	11. F	15. F	19. T
4. T	8. F	12. T	16. T	20. F

MULTIPLE-CHOICE QUIZ

1. d	4. e	7. c	10. a	13. b
2. e	5. c	8. e	11. a	14. d
3. e	6. b	9. e	12. d	15. c

SKILL-BUILDING QUIZ

INDICATIONS FROM SCORE:

90-100	Exceptional indications of entrepreneurial flair--you share most of the characteristics common to highly successful entrepreneurs.
75-89	Above-average indications of entrepreneurial flair--you share many of the characteristics common to highly successful entrepreneurs.
50-74	Average indications of entrepreneurial flair--you share some of the characteristics common to highly successful entrepreneurs.
0-49	Based on this analysis, it appears your chances of successfully starting an entrepreneurial business are marginal.

Chapter 7 Managerial Decision Making

CHAPTER OUTLINE

Introduction

Nature of Management

Management Functions
 Planning
 Organizing
 Staffing
 Directing
 Controlling

Types of Management
 Levels of Management
 Areas of Management

Skills Needed by Managers
 Leadership
 Technical Expertise
 Conceptual Skills
 Analytical Skills
 Human Relations Skills

Where Do Managers Come From?

Decision Making
 Recognizing and Defining the Decision Situation
 Developing Options
 Analyzing Options
 Selecting the Best Option
 Implementing the Decision
 Monitoring the Consequences

The Reality of Management

CHAPTER OBJECTIVES

After reading this chapter, you should be able to:
- Define management and explain its role in the achievement of organizational objectives.
- Describe the major functions of management.
- Distinguish among three levels of management and the concerns of managers at each level.
- Specify the skills managers need in order to be successful.
- Summarize the systematic approach to decision making used by many business managers.
- Recommend a new strategy to revive a struggling business.

Chapter 7 Managerial Decision Making

CHAPTER RECAP

NATURE OF MANAGEMENT

Management is a process designed to achieve an organization's objectives by using its resources effectively and efficiently in a changing environment. *Effectively* means having the intended result; *efficiently* means accomplishing the objectives with a minimum of resources. **Managers** make decisions about the use of the organization's resources and are concerned with planning, organizing, leading, and controlling the organization's activities so as to reach its objectives. Management takes place not only in businesses of all sizes, but in any organization requiring the coordination of resources. Every organization, in the pursuit of its objectives, must acquire resources (people, raw materials and equipment, money, and information) and coordinate their use to turn out a final good or service.

MANAGEMENT FUNCTIONS

To coordinate the use of resources so that the organization can develop, make, and sell products, managers engage in planning, organizing, staffing, directing, and controlling. These functions are interrelated, and managers may perform two or more of them at the same time.

Planning, the process of determining the organization's objectives and deciding how to accomplish them, lays the groundwork for the other functions. The plan specifies what should be done, by whom, where, when, and how. Businesses of all sizes need to develop plans for achieving success.

Objectives, the ends or results desired by the organization, derive from the organization's **mission**, which describes its fundamental purpose and basic philosophy. A business's objectives may be elaborate or simple; they usually relate to profit, competitive advantage, efficiency, and growth.

There are three general types of plans for meeting objectives--strategic, operational, and tactical. A firm's highest managers develop its **strategic plans**, which establish the long-range objectives and overall strategy or course of action for the firm to fulfill its mission and objectives. Strategic plans, which cover periods ranging from two to ten years or even longer, may include plans to add products, purchase companies, sell unprofitable segments of the business, issue stock, or move into international markets. **Tactical plans** are shorter-range plans designed to implement the activities and objectives specified in the strategic plan. These plans, which cover a period of one year or less, help keep the firm on the course established in the strategic plan. **Operational plans** are very short term and specify what actions specific individuals, work groups, or departments need to accomplish to achieve the tactical plan and, ultimately, the strategic plan. Another element in planning is **crisis management or contingency planning**, which deals with potential disasters such as product tampering, oil spills, earthquakes, or other disasters. Crisis management plans usually specify how to maintain business operations throughout a crisis and communicate with the public, employees, and officials about the problem and the company's response.

Organizing is the structuring of resources and activities to accomplish objectives efficiently and effectively. Managers organize by reviewing plans and determining what activities are necessary to implement them; then, they divide the work into small units and assign it to specific individuals, groups, or departments. Organizing helps create synergy, establishes lines of authority, improves

Chapter 7 Managerial Decision Making

communication, helps avoid the duplication of resources, and can improve competitiveness by speeding up decision making.

Staffing is hiring people to carry out the work of the organization. Beyond recruiting people for positions within the firm, managers must determine what skills are needed for specific jobs, how to motivate and train employees to do their assigned jobs, how much to pay employees, what benefits to provide, and how to prepare employees for higher-level jobs in the firm at a later date.

Directing is motivating and leading employees to achieve organizational objectives. Managers motivate employees by providing incentives for them to do a good job.

Controlling is the process of evaluating and correcting activities to keep the organization on course. It involves measuring performance, comparing present performance with standards or objectives, identifying deviations from the standards, investigating the causes of deviations, and taking corrective action when necessary. Controlling and planning are closely linked. The control process also helps managers deal with problems arising outside the firm.

TYPES OF MANAGEMEN

Managers may be classified by level or area of specialization. There are three levels of management, forming a pyramid. **Top managers** include the president and other top executives, such as the chief executive officer (CEO), chief financial officer (CFO), and chief operations officer (COO), who have overall responsibility for the organization. Top managers spend most of their time planning and making the organization's strategic decisions. **Middle managers** are responsible for tactical planning that will implement the general guidelines established by top management. They are involved in the specific operations of the organization and spend more time organizing. **First-line managers** supervise workers and daily operations of the organization. They spend most of their time directing and controlling.

Financial managers deal with the organization's financial resources. **Production and operations managers** develop and administer the activities involved in transforming resources into goods, services, and ideas ready for the marketplace. **Human resources managers** handle the staffing function, determining the organization's human resource needs; recruiting and hiring new employees; developing and administering employee benefits, training, and performance appraisal programs; and dealing with government regulations concerning employment practices. **Marketing managers** are responsible for planning, pricing, and promoting products, and making them available to customers. **Administrative managers** do not specialize in any particular area but, rather, manage an entire business or major segment of a business.

SKILLS NEEDED BY MANAGERS

Managing effectively and efficiently requires leadership, technical expertise, conceptual skills, analytical skills, and human relations skills.

Leadership is the ability to influence employees to work toward organizational goals. Managers can often be classified as one of three types of leaders. Autocratic leaders make all the decisions and then tell employees what must be done and how to do it. Democratic leaders involve their employees in

Chapter 7 Managerial Decision Making

decisions. Free-rein leaders let their employees work without much interference. Which type is best depends on the employees' abilities, the manager's abilities, the situation and other factors.

Technical expertise is the specialized knowledge and training needed to perform a job. Managers need technical knowledge and skills related to their area of management. Today's managers are finding computer expertise to be a valuable skill.

Conceptual skills involve the ability to think in abstract terms, to see how parts fit together to form the whole. They also relate to the ability to think creatively. Managers at all levels and in all areas need conceptual skills, but none more so than top-level managers.

Analytical skills are the ability to identify relevant issues and recognize the degree of their importance, understand the relationships between issues, and perceive the underlying causes of a situation. All managers need to think logically, but this skill is probably most important for top-level managers.

Human relations skills are the ability to deal with people, both inside and outside the organization. People skills are especially important in organizations that provide services.

WHERE DO MANAGERS COME FROM?

An organization acquires managers by promoting employees within the organization, hiring employees from other organizations, and hiring employees out of schools and universities. Promoting people within the organization into management positions tends to increase motivation by showing employees that those who work hard and are competent can advance in the company. However, it is vital for companies to hire outside people from time to time to bring fresh ideas into the organization.

DECISION MAKING

Managers make many different kinds of decisions, and decision-making is important in all management functions and levels, whether the decisions are on a strategic, tactical, or operational level. A systematic approach using six steps usually leads to more effective decision-making.

The first step in decision-making requires recognizing and defining the situation, which may be either positive or negative. Situations requiring small-scale decisions often occur without warning; those requiring large-scale decisions usually are preceded by warning signals. The situation must be carefully defined before management can make a decision.

The next step involves developing a list of possible courses of action, both standard and creative. As a general rule, more time and expertise are devoted to the development stage of decision making when the decision is of major importance.

The third step in decision-making involves analyzing the practicality and appropriateness of each option. Management should consider both the consequences of each option and whether the options adequately address the decision situation.

The fourth step involves selecting the best option from among the list of options. This is often a subjective process because many situations do not lend themselves to mathematical analysis.

Chapter 7 Managerial Decision Making

The fifth step is implementing the decision. Implementation can be simple or fairly complex, depending on the situation. Effective implementation requires planning. Additionally, management should anticipate resistance from people within the organization and be ready to deal with unexpected consequences.

Finally, management must monitor the consequences of its decision: Did the decision accomplish the desired result? If not, management must analyze the situation to find out if the decision was the wrong one, if the situation changed, or if some other option should be implemented. The decision situation may have been incorrectly defined, or the results may not have had time to show up.

THE REALITY OF MANAGEMENT

Management is not a cut-and-dried process; it is a widely varying process for achieving organizational goals. Managers plan, organize, staff, direct, and control, but even those functions can be boiled down into two functions: figuring out what to do and getting things done. Managers spend as much as 75 percent of their time working with other people both inside and outside the organization. They spend a lot of time establishing and updating an **agenda**, a list of both specific and vague items covering short-term and long-term objectives that must be accomplished. They also spend a lot of time **networking**, building relationships and sharing information with colleagues who can help managers achieve the items on their agendas. Finally, managers spend a great deal of time confronting the complex and difficult challenges of the business world today, such as rapidly changing technology; increased scrutiny of individual and corporate ethics and social responsibility; the changing nature of the work force; laws and regulations; increased global competition and more challenging foreign markets; declining educational standards, which may limit the skills and knowledge of the future labour and customer pool; and making the best use of time itself.

ENHANCEMENT EXERCISES

1. Identify members of your group, teachers, employers, government, etc. and describe their leadership styles. Be sure to note what makes the leadership style work for them. Are the majority of people autocratic, democratic or free reign when dealing with others?

MATCHING QUIZ

Match each of the following statements with the correct key term.

a. mission
b. strategic plans
c. tactical plans
d. operational plans
e. contingency planning

_____1.   Short-range plans that spell out the implementation of the organization's long-term strategies for fulfilling its objectives.

_____2.   Plans that establish the organization's long-range objectives and overall strategy for the firm to fulfill its mission and objectives.

Chapter 7 Managerial Decision Making

_____3.   Plan that spells out the organization's fundamental purpose and basic philosophy.

_____4.   Plans that spell out how the organization will respond to potential disasters such as product tampering, oil spills, earthquakes, computer virus, or an airplane crash.

_____5.   Short-term plans that specify what actions specific individuals, work groups, or departments need to accomplish.

TRUE/FALSE QUIZ

Indicate whether each of the following statements is true or false.

_____1.   Government organizations have no need for management.

_____2.   Tactical plans are long-range plans developed by top management.

_____3.   Autocratic leaders tell employees what to do and how to do it.

_____4.   Managers are typically evaluated as to their effectiveness and efficiency.

_____5.   Democratic leadership is best for unskilled, unmotivated employees.

_____6.   Promoting managers from within the organization boosts employee morale.

_____7.   If the desired result of a decision does not occur, management must analyze the situation again.

_____8.   Hiring people to carry out the work of the organization is known as organizing.

_____9.   Managers must carefully coordinate the use of resources if they are to achieve the organization's objectives.

_____10.   Top managers spend most of their time directing employees.

_____11.   All managers perform all management functions in the same degree.

_____12.   Directing is of primary importance to middle managers because they deal with employees on a daily basis.

_____13.   Controlling and planning are closely linked.

_____14.   Managers need technical expertise so that they can train employees, answer questions, and provide guidance.

_____15.   Production managers are responsible for planning, pricing, promoting, and distributing products.

____16.   Administrative managers have no expertise in a particular area.

____17.   Management should include creative courses of action in its list of options in the decision-making process.

____18.   Conceptual skills include the ability to think creatively.

____19.   Situations requiring major decisions occur without warning.

____20.   Management is a cut-and-dried process, facilitated by networking.

MULTIPLE-CHOICE QUIZ

Choose the correct answer for each of the following questions.

____1.   Which of the following leadership styles is generally best for unskilled, unmotivated workers?
   a.   autocratic
   b.   democratic
   c.   republican
   d.   free-rein
   e.   automatic

____2.   Which of the following deals with employees in a formalized manner?
   a.   financial management
   b.   administrative management
   c.   production and operations management
   d.   human resources management
   e.   marketing management

____3.   Which of the following involves determining the organization's objectives and deciding how to accomplish them?
   a.   controlling
   b.   directing
   c.   staffing
   d.   organizing
   e.   planning

____4.   Which of the following skills relates to the use of computers in business today?
   a.   leadership
   b.   technical expertise
   c.   conceptual skills
   d.   human relations skills
   e.   inferential skills

Chapter 7 Managerial Decision Making

_____5.   Which of the following do middle managers spend most of their time doing?
   a.   controlling
   b.   directing
   c.   staffing
   d.   planning
   e.   organizing

_____6.   In which of the following decision-making stages does a manager try to determine why a result was not achieved?
   a.   recognizing and defining the situation
   b.   analyzing options
   c.   implementing the decision
   d.   monitoring the consequences
   e.   developing options

_____7.   Which of the following is the first step in making a decision?
   a.   recognizing and defining the situation
   b.   analyzing options
   c.   throwing darts at a dart board
   d.   selecting the best option
   e.   developing a list of possible courses of action

_____8.   Which of the following makes strategic decisions, such as whether to acquire another company or expand operations internationally?
   a.   staff management
   b.   top management
   c.   middle management
   d.   first-line management
   e.   all of the above

_____9.   Which of the following is NOT a limitation in the option-development stage of decision making?
   a.   legal restrictions
   b.   appropriateness
   c.   technology
   d.   the state of the economy
   e.   ethics

_____10.   Which of the following is NOT a common objective of a business?
   a.   profit
   b.   market share
   c.   toss
   d.   social responsibility
   e.   growth

Chapter 7 Managerial Decision Making

_____11.   Which of the following spend most of their time directing and controlling?
   a.   employees
   b.   first-line managers
   c.   middle managers
   d.   top managers
   e.   all of the above

_____12.   Which of the following is one of the steps in the control process?
   a.   motivating employees
   b.   evaluating managerial performance
   c.   identifying deviations from the standard
   d.   implementing the decision
   e.   recognizing and defining a decision situation

_____13.   Which of the following is NOT a specific function of management?
   a.   marketing
   b.   controlling
   c.   directing
   d.   planning
   e.   organizing

_____14.   Which of the following skills relates to getting along with others?
   a.   leadership
   b.   conceptual skills
   c.   human relations skills
   d.   inferential skills
   e.   technical skills

_____15.   Which of the following do top managers spend most of their time doing?
   a.   controlling
   b.   directing
   c.   staffing
   d.   planning
   e.   organizing

Ferrell, Hirt, Bates & Currie, Business: A Changing World, First Edition

Chapter 7 Managerial Decision Making

SKILL-BUILDING QUIZ

In the "Build Your Skills" exercise of your text, you practiced recognizing the various management functions and seeing how they are interrelated. Build on that exercise by choosing the correct answer for each of the following.

_____1.   One of your employees has come to you--the shop-floor supervisor in a small manufacturing firm--asking permission to stop the line to determine why the products in the most recent batch are coming out with major defects. Although you will exercise several of the management functions, which of the following best describes the management function you will employ to resolve this issue?
   a.   planning
   b.   organizing
   c.   staffing
   d.   directing
   e.   controlling

_____2.   You are a manager at a small manufacturing firm facing quality problems. On exploring the issue, you find that employee morale is quite low, and they simply don't care about quality. Which of the following best describes the management function you need to engage in to resolve the issue?
   a.   planning
   b.   organizing
   c.   staffing
   d.   directing
   e.   controlling

_____3.   Because the restaurant you own has been so successful, you have decided to open a new restaurant on the other side of town. You are currently making decisions about the location of the new facility, whether it will be identical to the present one or different, and whom to hire as the head chef. Which of the following best describes the management function you are using?
   a.   planning
   b.   organizing
   c.   staffing
   d.   directing
   e.   controlling

Chapter 7 Managerial Decision Making

_____ 4.   As owner of a successful, long-lived restaurant business, you have just learned that one of your chefs plans to retire. You have recently learned that another of your restaurant's chefs lied on his resume and actually never went to the cooking school he claimed to have attended, although he is a more-than-adequate chef. In deciding how to handle these situations, which of the following best describes the management function you are using?
   a.   planning
   b.   organizing
   c.   staffing
   d.   directing
   e.   controlling

ANSWERS

MATCHING QUIZ

1. c   2. b   3. a   4. e   5. d

TRUE/FALSE QUIZ

1. F	5. F	9. T	13. T	17. T
2. F	6. T	10. F	14. T	18. T
3. T	7. T	11. F	15. F	19. F
4. T	8. F	12. F	16. F	20. F

MULTIPLE-CHOICE QUIZ

1. a	4. b	7. a	10. c	13. a
2. d	5. e	8. b	11. b	14. c
3. e	6. d	9. b	12. c	15. d

SKILL-BUILDING QUIZ

1. e   2. d   3. a   4. c

Ferrell, Hirt, Bates & Currie, Business: A Changing World, First Edition

Chapter 8 Organization, Teamwork, and Communication

CHAPTER OUTLINE

Introduction

Developing Organizational Structure

Specialization

Departmentalization
       Functional Departmentalization
       Product Departmentalization
       Geographical Departmentalization
       Customer Departmentalization

The Role of Groups and Teams in Organizations
       Benefits of Teams
       Types of Groups

Assigning Responsibility and Delegating Authority
       Delegation of Authority
       Degree of Centralization
       Span of Management
       Downsizing Organizations

Forms of Organizational Structure
       Line Structure
       Line-and-Staff Structure
       Multidivisional Structure
       Matrix Structure

Communicating in Organizations
       Formal Communication
       Informal Communication Channels

Organizational Culture

Chapter 8 Organization, Teamwork, and Communication

CHAPTER OBJECTIVES

After reading this chapter, you should be able to:
- Define organizational structure and relate how organizational structures develop.
- Describe how specialization and departmentalization help an organization achieve its goals.
- Distinguish between groups and teams and identify the types of groups that exist in organizations.
- Determine how organizations assign responsibility for tasks and delegate authority.
- Compare and contrast some common forms of organizational structure.
- Describe how communication occurs in organizations.
- Analyze a business's use of teams.

CHAPTER RECAP

DEVELOPING ORGANIZATIONAL STRUCTURE

Rarely is an organization, or any group of individuals working together, able to achieve common objectives without some form of structure, whether that structure is explicitly defined or only implied. **Structure** is the arrangement or relationship of positions within an organization. An organization's structure develops when managers assign work tasks and activities to specific individuals and work groups and coordinate the diverse activities required to reach the firm's objectives. Growth requires organizing--the structuring of human, physical, and financial resources to achieve objectives efficiently and effectively.

SPECIALIZATION

An organization must first determine what activities are required to achieve its objectives and then break these activities down into specific tasks that can be handled by individual employees. This division of labour into small, specific tasks and the assignment of employees to do a single task is called **specialization**. The rationale for specialization is efficiency: It minimizes the time lost when workers shift from one task to another, and it facilitates training. It may be necessary when the activities to be performed are too numerous for one person. Overspecialization can have negative consequences, such as employee boredom and dissatisfaction.

DEPARTMENTALIZATION

After assigning specialized tasks to individuals, managers next organize workers doing similar jobs into groups to make them easier to manage. **Departmentalization** is the grouping of jobs into working units called departments, units, groups, or divisions. Most companies use more than one method of departmentalization to enhance productivity. **Functional departmentalization** groups together jobs that perform similar functional activities--such as finance, manufacturing, marketing, and human resources--with each group managed by an expert in that function. **Product departmentalization** organizes jobs around the products of the firm. **Geographical departmentalization** groups jobs according to geographic location, such as a provincial, region, country, or continent. **Customer departmentalization** arranges jobs around the needs of various types of customers. Each of these departmentalization methods has advantages and disadvantages.

Chapter 8 Organization, Teamwork, and Communication

THE ROLE OF GROUPS AND TEAMS IN ORGANIZATIONS

Regardless of how they are organized, most of the essential work of business occurs in individual work groups and teams. A **group** has traditionally been defined as two or more individuals who communicate with one another, share a common identity, and have a common goal. However, businesses are moving toward greater use of teams, which are small groups whose members have complementary skills; a common purpose, goals, and approach; and who hold themselves mutually accountable. All teams are groups, but not all groups are teams. A work group's performance depends on what its members do as individuals, while a team's performance is based on collective products.

Teams are becoming more common as businesses try to boost productivity and become more competitive. Teams can pool and make greater use of members' knowledge and skills than can individuals working alone; create more solutions for solving problems than can individuals; enhance employee acceptance of, understanding of, and commitment to team goals; motivate and involve workers; boost innovativeness and productivity; and reduce costs.

The type of groups an organization establishes depends on the tasks it needs to accomplish and the situation it faces. A **committee** is usually a permanent formal group that does same specific task. A **task force** is a temporary group of employees--who typically come from across all departments and levels of an organization--responsible for bringing about a particular change. **Project teams** are similar to task forces, but normally they actually run their operation and have total control of a specific work project. **Product-development teams** are a special type of project team formed to devise, design, and implement a new product. **Quality-assurance teams** (or **quality circles**) are fairly small groups of workers brought together from throughout the organization to solve specific quality, productivity and service problems. A **self-directed work team (SDWT)** is group of employees responsible for an entire work process or segment that delivers a product to an internal or external customer.

ASSIGNING RESPONSIBILITY AND DELEGATING AUTHORITY

After workers have been organized into groups and assigned their tasks, they must be given the responsibility to carry out their assigned activities. Management must determine the extent to which responsibility will be delegated throughout the organization, the chain of command of authority, and how many employees will report to each manager.

Delegation of authority gives not only tasks to employees, but also the power to make commitments, use resources, and take whatever actions are necessary to carry out those tasks. Delegation gives a **responsibility**, or obligation, on employees to carry out assigned tasks satisfactorily and holds them accountable for the proper execution of their assigned work. The principle of **accountability** means that employees who accept an assignment and the authority to carry it out are answerable to a superior for the outcome. The process of delegating authority establishes a pattern of relationships and accountability between superior and subordinates. These authority and responsibility relationships are often shown graphically on an **organizational chart** showing organizational structure, lines of authority (chain of command), staff relationships, permanent committee assignments, and lines of communication.

Chapter 8 Organization, Teamwork, and Communication

The extent to which authority is delegated throughout an organization determines its degree of centralization. In a **centralized organization**, authority is concentrated at the top, and very little decision-making authority is delegated to lower levels. Businesses tend to be more centralized when the decisions to be made are risky and when low-level managers are not highly skilled in decision making. Overcentralization can cause serious problems for a company, in part, because it may take longer for the organization as a whole to implement decisions and to respond to changes and problems on a regional scale. A **decentralized organization** is one in which decision-making authority is delegated as far down the chain of command as possible. Decentralization is characteristic of organizations that operate in complex, unpredictable environments. Delegating authority to lower levels of managers may increase a firm's productivity.

Experts suggest that top managers should not directly supervise more than four to eight people, while lower-level managers who supervise routine tasks are capable of managing a much larger number of subordinates. **Span of management** refers to the number of subordinates who report to a particular manager. A wide span of management exists when a manager directly supervises a large number of employees; a narrow span exists when a manager directly supervises only a few subordinates. A narrow span of management is appropriate when superiors and subordinates are not in close proximity, the manager has many responsibilities in addition to supervising, interaction between superiors and subordinates is frequent, and problems are common. A wide span of management is appropriate when superiors and subordinates are located close to one another, the manager has few responsibilities other than supervision, the level of interaction between superiors and subordinates is low, few problems arise, subordinates are highly competent, and a set of specific operating procedures governs everyone's activities. Narrow spans of management are typical in centralized organizations, while wide spans of management are more common in decentralized firms.

Organizational layers refer to the levels of management in an organization. Tall organizations have many layers of management and narrow spans of management. Because managers supervise fewer employees, administrative costs are higher and decision making is slower. Flat organizations have fewer levels of management and wide spans of management. These managers have more administrative duties and spend more time supervising.

Downsizing is the elimination of significant numbers of employees from an organization. It makes tall organizations flatter as companies lay off large numbers of employees, widen spans of management, and decentralize to reduce costs and increase responsiveness and creativity in the face of increasing global competition. Downsizing has both positive and negative consequences, making it a controversial practice.

FORMS OF ORGANIZATIONAL STRUCTURE

Along with assigning tasks and the responsibility for carrying them out, managers must consider how to structure their authority relationships--that is, what structure the organization itself will have, how it will appear on the organizational chart.

The simplest organizational structure, **line structure**, has direct lines of authority that extend from the top manager to employees at the lowest level of the organization. This structure has a clear chain of command, enabling managers to make decisions quickly, but requires that managers possess a wide range of knowledge. Line structures are most common in small businesses.

Chapter 8 Organization, Teamwork, and Communication

The **line-and-staff structure** has a traditional line relationship between superiors and subordinates, and specialized managers--called staff managers--are available to assist line managers. Line managers focus on their area of expertise, while staff managers provide advice and support to line departments on specialized matters. This structure may result in overstaffing and ambiguous lines of communication.

A **multidivisional structure** groups departments together into larger groups called divisions, organized on the basis of geography, customer, product, or a combination. Multidivisional structures permit delegation of decision-making authority, allowing divisional and department managers to specialize. They allow better, faster, more innovative decisions and help each division focus on the unique needs of its customers. However, the divisional structure creates duplication of resources.

A **matrix structure**, also called a project-management structure, sets up teams from different departments, thereby creating two or more intersecting lines of authority. Project departments are superimposed on the more traditional, function-based departments. These structures are generally temporary. Matrix structures provide flexibility, enhanced cooperation and creativity, and responsiveness, but they are generally expensive and quite complex.

COMMUNICATING IN ORGANIZATIONS

Communication within an organization can flow in a variety of directions and from a number of sources, using both oral and written communication forms. There are both formal and informal communication flows within organizations.

Formal channels of communication are intentionally defined and designed by the organization. They represent the flow of communication within the formal organizational structure, as shown on organizational charts. Formal communication may flow upward, downward, horizontally, and diagonally.

Along with the formal channels of communication shown on an organizational chart, all firms communicate informally as well, through friendships and other nonwork social relationships. The most significant informal communication occurs through the **grapevine**, an informal channel of communication, separate from management's formal, official communication channels. Information passed along the grapevine may relate to the job or organization, or it may be gossip and rumors unrelated to either, and it may be surprisingly accurate. Managers can use the grapevine to their advantage.

ORGANIZATIONAL CULTURE

Organizational culture, also called corporate culture, refers to the organization's shared values, beliefs, traditions, philosophies, rules, and heroes. It gives the members of an organization meaning and suggests rules for how to behave and deal with problems within the organization. It may be expressed formally through codes of ethics, memos, manuals, and ceremonies, but it is more often expressed informally through dress codes, work habits, extracurricular activities, and stories.

Chapter 8 Organization, Teamwork, and Communication

ENHANCEMENT EXERCISES

1. Divide into groups of three or more people. Each group should have an unlimited supply of paper clips and a marble or a small ball. The task is to build a ramp from the top of the desk to the floor on which the marble can roll. After, write a reflection on the assignment – describe how you completed the task, whether anyone took a leadership role and how the team worked together to form a solution.

MATCHING QUIZ

Match the following statements with the correct key term.

a. line structure
b. functional departmentalization
c. line-and-staff structure
d. multidivisional structure
e. matrix structure

_____1.   In this organization type, jobs that perform similar activities, such as finance, marketing, or human resources, are grouped.

_____2.   In this structure, direct lines of authority extend from the top manager to employees at the lowest level of the organization.

_____3.   In this structure, departments are grouped together into larger groups called divisions.

_____4.   In this structure, teams are set up from different departments, thereby creating two or more intersecting lines of authority.

_____5.   In this structure, there is a traditional relationship between superiors and subordinates, and specialized managers are available to assist line managers.

TRUE/FALSE QUIZ

Indicate whether each of the following statements is true or false.

_____1.   Customer departmentalization allows an organization to respond to the needs of different groups of customers.

_____2.   Tall organizations generally have wide spans of management and low administrative costs.

_____3.   A multidivisional structure is based on direct lines of authority that extend from the top executive to the lowest level of the organization, allowing managers to make quick decisions.

Chapter 8 Organization, Teamwork, and Communication

_____4.   Project teams normally run their own operations and have total control of a specific work project.

_____5.   An organization can achieve its objectives without structure.

_____6.   Delegation of authority frees a manager to concentrate on larger issues, such as planning or dealing with problems and opportunities.

_____7.   A task force is a temporary group of employees brought together from throughout the organization to solve specific quality, productivity, or service problems.

_____8.   Specialization is the grouping of jobs into working units called departments, units, groups, or divisions.

_____9.   Downsizing makes tall organizations flatter as companies lay off employees, widen spans of management, and decentralize.

_____10.   Delegation establishes a pattern of relationships and accountability between managers and subordinates.

_____11.   Organizations tend to centralize when risky decisions must be made and when low-level managers are not skilled decision makers.

_____12.   The grapevine is a channel of communication that is intentionally defined and designed by the organization.

_____13.   All teams are groups.

_____14.   Managers should not supervise more than eight people.

_____15.   The rationale for specialization is efficiency.

_____16.   A weakness of functional departmentalization is that it tends to emphasize departmental units rather than the organization as a whole, slowing decision making that involves more than one department.

_____17.   Adam Smith described departmentalization in _The Wealth of Nations_.

_____18.   A wide span of management is most appropriate when a manager has many responsibilities in addition to supervision, managers and subordinates are far apart, and there are many problems.

_____19.   Matrix structures allow an organization to respond quickly to changes in the market.

_____20.   Organizational culture refers to the personal and social relationships that evolve in the work environment.

Chapter 8 Organization, Teamwork, and Communication

MULTIPLE-CHOICE QUIZ

Choose the correct answer for each of the following questions.

_____1.   Which of the following is NOT usually a characteristic of a flat organization?
- a. wide span of management
- b. higher administrative costs
- c. few organizational layers
- d. faster communication
- e. less interaction between managers and subordinates

_____2.   When team members from diverse departments and different levels communicate with each other, it is an example of
- a. upward communication.
- b. downward communication.
- c. diagonal communication.
- d. horizontal communication.
- e. the grapevine.

_____3.   Which departmentalization method works best when activities related to specific products must be coordinated?
- a. product departmentalization
- b. territorial departmentalization
- c. customer departmentalization
- d. line-and-staff departmentalization
- e. functional departmentalization

_____4.   Which of the following is the first step in organizing?
- a. Give workers and work groups the responsibility and authority to carry out their assigned tasks.
- b. Organize workers doing similar jobs into groups to make them easier to manage.
- c. Determine what activities are necessary to achieve the organization's objectives.
- d. Break down activities into specific tasks and assign these tasks to individuals.
- e. Organize work groups into divisions.

_____5.   Which of the following is a reason for centralizing an organization?
- a. diverse, unpredictable markets
- b. managers must make risky decisions
- c. low-level managers are skilled decision makers
- d. an active grapevine
- e. organizations should not be centralized

Chapter 8 Organization, Teamwork, and Communication

_____6.   Which of the following is NOT a potential consequence of overspecialization?
     a.   boredom
     b.   injuries
     c.   poor quality
     d.   efficiency
     e.   high turnover

_____7.   Which of the following is a method of departmentalization?
     a.   customer departmentalization
     b.   line departmentalization
     c.   matrix departmentalization
     d.   centralized departmentalization
     e.   formal departmentalization

_____8.   Which of the following is a permanent formal group that does some specific task?
     a.   quality circle
     b.   self-directed work team
     c.   project team
     d.   committee
     e.   task force

_____9.   When friends who work on different teams talk to each other about a coworker's relationship with another coworker, it is an example of which kind of communication?
     a.   upward
     b.   downward
     c.   horizontal
     d.   diagonal
     e.   the grapevine

_____10.   All of the following apply to a newly downsized organization, EXCEPT
     a.   decentralized decision making.
     b.   flat organization.
     c.   wide span of management.
     d.   narrow span of management.
     e.   low morale.

_____11.   Which of the following structures is most often used in a small business?
     a.   line structure
     b.   functional structure
     c.   matrix structure
     d.   line-and-staff structure
     e.   task force

Chapter 8 Organization, Teamwork, and Communication

____12.   A group of employees responsible for an entire work process or segment that delivers a product to an internal or external customer is a
   a. project team.
   b. self-directed work team.
   c. product-development team.
   d. task force.
   e. committee.

____13.   Which of the following is NOT a reason for having a wide span of management?
   a. Managers have few responsibilities other than supervision.
   b. The level of interaction between superiors and subordinates is low.
   c. Subordinates are highly competent.
   d. Problems are common.
   e. A set of specific operating procedures governs the activities of managers and their subordinates.

____14.   Which of the following structures allows a business to respond quickly to changes by giving special attention to specific projects or problems?
   a. line
   b. functional structure
   c. matrix structure
   d. line-and-staff structure
   e. task force

____15.   Which departmentalization method works best when an organization's customers have different needs?
   a. product departmentalization
   b. territorial departmentalization
   c. customer departmentalization
   d. line-and-staff departmentalization
   e. marketing departmentalization

Chapter 8 Organization, Teamwork, and Communication

SKILL-BUILDING QUIZ

In the "Build Your Skills" exercise of your text, you practiced recognizing the characteristics of teamwork. Continue building on those skills by honing your understanding of the various types of groups and teams discussed in the chapter. Choose the correct answer for each of the following questions.

_____1.   You are a member of a permanent group that addresses ethical concerns within your company. The group, which includes the company president, has, over the years of its existence, drafted a code of ethics, formulated a policy for enforcing the code, and implemented and currently oversees a hotline for employees to call with ethical questions and problems. Which of the following best describes the group?
   a.   committee
   b.   project team
   c.   quality-assurance team
   d.   self-directed work team
   e.   task force

_____2.   You have been assigned to be a member of a temporary group which includes members from marketing, finance, operations, and management, as well as a customer, to find ways to speed up the process of getting your company's product to the customer. Which of the following best describes the group?
   a.   committee
   b.   project team
   c.   quality-assurance team
   d.   self-directed work team
   e.   task force

_____3.   You work in the marketing department of a consumer-products firm. You have just been assigned to be a member of a group formed to devise, design, and set up production for a new high-tech product. The team includes members from marketing, operations, management, and finance. Which of the following best describes the group?
   a.   task force
   b.   project team
   c.   product-development team
   d.   self-directed work team
   e.   quality-assurance teem

Chapter 8 Organization, Teamwork, and Communication

_____ 4.   At an automobile manufacturing firm, you have just been assigned to be a member of a group of employees who are responsible for every aspect of assembling the rear end of your company's best-selling pickup truck and sending it to the next phase of manufacturing. Because you are responsible for every aspect of this process, you will be able to, if necessary, shut down the assembly line to solve problems. Team members, who will be fully cross-trained, will rotate among the various tasks involved in completing the process, including the role of team leader. You will also be responsible for scheduling and managing the inventory needed to carry out your responsibility. Which of the following best describes your group?
   a.   task force
   b.   project team
   c.   product-development team.
   d.   self-directed work team
   e.   quality-assurance team

ANSWERS

MATCHING QUIZ

1. b   2. a   3. d   4. e   5. c

TRUE/FALSE QUIZ

1. T	5. F	9. T	13. T	17. F
2. F	6. T	10. T	14. F	18. F
3. F	7. F	11. T	15. T	19. T
4. T	8. F	12. F	16. T	20. F

MULTIPLE-CHOICE QUIZ

1. b	4. c	7. a	10. d	13. d
2. c	5. b	8. d	11. a	14. c
3. a	6. d	9. e	12. b	15. c

SKILL-BUILDING QUIZ

1. a   2. e   3. c   4. d

Chapter 9 Production and Operations Management

CHAPTER OUTLINE

Introduction

The Nature of Operations Management
  The Transformation Process
  Operations Management in Service Businesses

Planning and Designing Operations Systems
  Planning the Product
  Designing the Operations Processes
  Planning Capacity
  Planning Facilities

Managing Logistics
  Purchasing
  Managing Inventory
  Routing and Scheduling

Managing Quality
  Establishing Standards--ISO 9000
  Inspection
  Sampling

CHAPTER OBJECTIVES

After reading this chapter, you should be able to:
* Define operations management and differentiate between operations and manufacturing.
* Explain how operations management differs in manufacturing and service firms.
* Describe the elements involved in planning and designing an operations system.
* Specify some techniques managers may use to manage the logistics of transforming inputs into finished products.
* Assess the importance of quality in operations management.
* Evaluate a business's dilemma and propose a solution.

CHAPTER RECAP

INTRODUCTION

All organizations create products for customers, and they often use similar processes to transform resources into goods, services, and ideas.

THE NATURE OF OPERATIONS MANAGEMENT

Operations management (OM), the development and administration of the activities involved in transforming resources into goods and services, is of critical importance in business. Operations managers oversee the transformation process and the planning and designing of operations systems,

Chapter 9 Production and Operations Management

managing logistics, quality, and productivity. OM is the "core" of most organizations because it is responsible for the creation of their products. OM has historically been called "production" or "manufacturing" because of the view that it was limited to the manufacture of physical goods. The trend to call it "operations" instead recognizes the growing importance of organizations that provide services and ideas. We use the terms **manufacturing** and **production** interchangeably to represent the activities and processes used in making tangible products, whereas we use the broader term **operations** to describe those processes used in the making of both tangible and intangible products.

The heart of operations management is the transformation process through which **inputs** (resources such as labour, money, materials, energy) are converted into **outputs** (goods, services, and ideas). The transformation process combines inputs in predetermined ways using different equipment, administrative procedures, and technology to create a product. Transformation may take place through one or more processes.

Transformation processes occur in all organizations, regardless of their output or objectives. Though manufacturers and service providers often perform similar activities, they also differ in several respects. First, they differ in the nature and consumption of their output: A manufacturer makes tangible products, whereas a service provider produces more intangible outputs. The service provider's product requires a higher degree of customer contact, and the actual performance of the service typically occurs at the point of consumption. Thus, service providers are often more limited in selecting work methods, assigning jobs, scheduling work, and exercising control over operations. A second way to classify differences between manufacturers and service providers has to do with the uniformity of inputs: Manufacturers typically have more control over the variability of the resources they use than do service providers. The products of service organizations tend to be more "customized." Manufacturers and service providers also differ in the uniformity of their output: Because of the human element inherent in providing services, each service tends to be performed differently. A fourth point of difference is the amount of labour required: Service providers are generally more labour-intensive because of the high level of customer contact, perishability of the output, and high degree of variation of inputs and outputs. The final distinction between service providers and manufacturers involves the measurement of productivity for each output produced. For the service provider, variations in demand, variations in service requirements from job to job, and the intangibility of the product make productivity measurement more difficult. In reality, most organizations are a combination of manufacturer and service provider, with both tangible and intangible qualities embodied in what they produce. The level of tangibility greatly influences the nature of the firm's operational processes and procedures.

PLANNING AND DESIGNING OPERATIONS SYSTEMS

The operations planning process usually involves all departments, not just operations management.

Before making any product, a company must first determine what consumers want and then design a product to satisfy that want. Most companies use marketing research to determine the kinds of goods and services to produce and the features they must possess. After developing an idea for a product, the engineering or research and development department converts it into a workable design and determines how best to produce it. Finally, operations managers must plan for the types and quantities of materials needed to produce the product, the skills and quantity of people needed to make the product, as well as the actual transformation processes.

Chapter 9 Production and Operations Management

Before a firm can begin production, it must first determine the appropriate method of transforming resources into the desired product. Often, consumer needs dictate the process. Products are typically designed to be manufactured by one of three processes. **Standardization** is making identical, interchangeable components or even complete products. Standardization speeds up production and quality control and reduces production costs, but customers may not get exactly what they want. **Modular design** involves building an item in self-contained units, or modules, that can be combined or interchanged to create different products. While this process allows products to be repaired quickly, the components themselves are usually expensive. **Customization** is making products to meet a particular customer's needs or wants.

Next, planners consider **capacity,** which basically refers to the maximum load that an organizational unit can carry or operate. Capacity levels that fall short can result in unmet demand, while excessive capacity can drive up operating costs due to unused and often expensive resources.

After determining what process will be used to create its products, the firm can then design and build an appropriate facility in which to make them. Facility location is an important issue because once the decision is made to locate in a specific area, the firm is stuck with the decision. The criteria an organization must consider when making a location decision vary from industry to industry, but all organizations consider proximity to the market; availability of raw materials, transportation power, and labor; climatic influences; community characteristics; and taxes and inducements in their facility-location decision. This complex decision requires the evaluation of many factors, some of which cannot be precisely measured.

Arranging the physical layout of a facility is a complex, highly technical task. Three basic layouts are common, but most firms use a combination of layout designs. A company using a **fixed-position layout** brings all resources required to create the product to a central location. Such a company may be called a **project organization** because it is typically involved in large, complex projects such as construction or exploration. Firms that use a **process layout** organize the transformation process into departments that group related processes. These types of organizations are sometimes called **intermittent organizations,** which deal with products of a lesser magnitude than do project organizations, and their products not necessarily unique but possess a significant number of differences. The **product layout** requires that production be broken down into relatively simple tasks assigned to workers, who are usually positioned along an assembly line. Companies that use assembly lines are usually known as **continuous manufacturing organizations,** so named because once they are set up, they run continuously, creating products with many similar characteristics.

Every industry has a basic, underlying technology that dictates the nature of its transformation process. Two technologies that have strongly influenced the operations of many organizations are computers and robotics. **Computer-assisted design (CAD)** helps engineers design components, products, and processes on computer instead of paper. **Computer-assisted manufacturing (CAM)** goes a step further, employing specialized computer systems to actually guide and control the transformation processes. Such systems can monitor the transformation process, gathering information about the equipment used to produce the products and about the product itself as it goes from one stage of the transformation process to the next. In **flexible manufacturing,** computers can direct machinery to adapt to different versions of similar operations. Robots are also becoming increasingly useful in the transformation process, especially in automobile manufacturing and nuclear waste cleanup. When CAD/CAM, flexible manufacturing, robotics, computer systems, and other technologies are

Chapter 9 Production and Operations Management

integrated, the result is **computer-integrated manufacturing (CIM),** a complete system that designs products, manages machines and materials, and controls the operations function.

MANAGING LOGISTICS

Logistics, a major function of operations, refers to all the activities involved in obtaining and managing raw materials and component parts, managing finished products, packaging them, and getting them to customers.

Purchasing, or procurement, is the buying of all the materials needed by the organization. The purchasing department aims to obtain items of the desired quality in the right quantities at the lowest possible cost. The purchasing department locates and evaluates suppliers for the raw materials, parts, components, manufacturing and office supplies, and equipment the firm requires. The purchasing function can be quite complex. Not all organizations purchase all the materials needed to create their products; sometimes they make or lease them.

Every raw material, component, completed or partially completed product, and piece of equipment a firm uses--its **inventory**--must be accounted for, or controlled. **Inventory control** is the process of determining how many supplies and goods are needed and keeping track of quantities on hand, where each item is, and who is responsible for it. Managing operations must be closely coordinated with inventory control. Inventory managers spend a great deal of time trying to determine the proper inventory level for each item, considering variables such as the usage rate of the item, the cost of maintaining the item in inventory, the cost of paperwork and other procedures associated with ordering or making the item, and the cost of the item itself. One popular approach is the **economic order quantity (EOQ) model,** which identifies the optimum number of items to order to minimize the costs of managing (ordering, storing, and using) them. An increasingly popular technique is **just-in-time (JIT) inventory management,** which eliminates waste by using smaller quantities of materials that arrive "just in time" for use in the transformation process and, therefore, require less storage space and other inventory management expense. Another inventory **management technique is material-requirements planning (MRP),** a planning system that schedules the precise quantity of materials needed to make the product.

After all materials have been procured and their use determined, managers must then consider the **routing,** or sequence of operations through which the product must pass. **Scheduling** then assigns the tasks to be done to departments or even specific machines, workers, or teams. One popular scheduling method is the *Program Evaluation and Review Technique (PERT),* which identifies all the major activities or events required to complete a project, arranges them in a sequence or path, determines the critical path, and estimates the time required for each event. If any activities on the critical path fall behind schedule, the entire project will be delayed.

MANAGING QUALITY

Controlling quality is another critical element in production and operations management because defective products can harm a firm. Quality reflects the degree to which a good or service meets the demands and requirements of customers. Determining quality can be difficult because it depends on customers' perceptions of how well the product meets or exceeds their expectations. **Quality control** refers to the processes an organization uses to maintain its established quality standards. Companies employing **total quality management (TQM)** programs know that quality control must be

Chapter 9 Production and Operations Management

incorporated throughout the transformation process, from the initial plans to develop a specific product through the facility planning stages to the actual manufacture of the product. One method through which many companies have tried to improve quality is **statistical process control,** a system in which management collects and analyzes information about the production process to pinpoint quality problems in the production system.

Regardless of whether a company has a TQM program to control quality, it must first determine what standard of quality is desired and then assess whether its products meet that standard. Both manufacturing and service-providing firms must set product specifications and quality standards. **ISO 9000** is a series of quality assurance standards designed to ensure consistent product quality under many conditions. Inspection reveals whether a product meets quality standards. Some product characteristics can be discerned by simple inspection techniques, such as weighing or measuring; others are more elaborate. Inspection is made of purchased items, work-in-process and finished items. Whether to inspect 100 percent of the output or to sample only part of it depends on the cost of the inspection process, its destructiveness, and the importance of the item to the safety of consumers or others. Using statistical inference, management can structure sampling techniques to assure a high probability of rejecting a population that does not meet standards and accepting a population that does. Sampling is likely to be used when inspection tests are destructive.

ENHANCEMENT EXERCISES

The ISO 9000 designation is very well known and increasingly widespread. Break into groups and conduct a debate whether the time spent attaining the designation is worthwhile for a company, city or community. Prior to the debate it would be helpful to learn more about the designation by using the World Wide Web.

MATCHING QUIZ

Match the following statements with the correct key term.

a. computer-assisted design (CAD)
b. computer-assisted manufacturing (CAM)
c. flexible manufacturing
d. computer-integrated manufacturing (CIM)

_____1.	A system in which computers direct machinery to adapt to different versions of similar operations.

_____2.	A system that designs products, manages machines and materials, and controls the operations function.

_____3.	The use of specialized computer systems to actually guide and control the transformation processes.

_____4.	The design of components, products, and processes on computer instead of paper.

Chapter 9 Production and Operations Management

TRUE/FALSE QUIZ

Indicate whether each of the following statements is true or false.

_____1.   Customization is making products according to agreed to specifications so that their parts are interchangeable.

_____2.   Because of their high level of customer contact, service providers are often more limited than manufacturers in selecting work methods, assigning jobs, scheduling work, and exercising control over operations.

_____3.   Flexible manufacturing allows computers to direct machinery to adapt to different versions of similar operations.

_____4.   All organizations use just one facility layout.

_____5.   The transformation process occurs only in organizations that manufacture goods.

_____6.   Material-requirements planning (MRP) is a computerized system that identifies the optimum number of items to order to minimize the costs of managing them.

_____7.   The purpose of inspecting work-in-process is to find defects before the product is completed so that they can be corrected.

_____8.   An assembly line is an example of a process layout.

_____9.   On a Program Evaluation and Review Technique (PERT) diagram, a critical path is a completed activity.

_____10.   Service providers are generally more labour-intensive than manufacturers because of their high level of customer contact, perishability of the output, and high degree of variation of inputs and outputs.

_____11.   Operations, production, and manufacturing can all be used interchangeably because they mean the same thing.

_____12.   Determining quality can be difficult because it depends on customers' perceptions of how well the product meets or exceeds their expectations.

_____13.   Statistical process control is a quality-improvement method in which management collects and analyzes information about the production process to pinpoint quality problems.

_____14.   Inventory control minimizes the number of units in inventory by providing an almost continuous flow of items from suppliers.

_____15.   Standardization speeds up production and quality control and reduces production costs.

Chapter 9 Production and Operations Management

_____16. Project organizations manufacture standardized products.

_____17. Organizations using the just-in-time concept must have extremely reliable suppliers located nearby.

_____18. Routing is assigning the work to be done to departments or specific machines.

_____19. Climate is an important consideration in the decision on where to locate an organization's facilities.

_____20. Some computer systems can take corrective action when equipment or certain product characteristics do not conform to predetermined standards.

MULTIPLE-CHOICE QUIZ

Choose the correct answer for each of the following questions.

_____1. Which of the following is the sequence of operations through which a product must pass?
   a. scheduling
   b. sequencing
   c. logistics
   d. purchasing
   e. routing

_____2. In which of the following does the product not move?
   a. process layout
   b. fixed-position layout
   c. intermittent organization
   d. product layout
   e. continuous manufacturing organization

_____3. Which of the following was NOT cited in your text as a criterion for deciding where to locate a facility?
   a. proximity to market
   b. availability of raw materials
   c. availability of power
   d. federal government regulations
   e. community characteristics

_____4. Which of the following is the buying of all materials needed by the organization?
   a. inventory control
   b. procurement
   c. routing
   d. scheduling

e. logistics

____5. Which of the following refers to the processes an organization uses to maintain its established quality standards?
a. logistics
b. sampling
c. inspection
d. statistical process control
e. quality control

____6. Which of the following creates products with many similar characteristics?
a. process layout
b. fixed-position layout
c. project organization
d. continuous manufacturing organization
e. intermittent organization

____7. Scheduling is
a. assigning the work to be done to departments or even specific machines.
b. the sequence of operations through which the product must pass.
c. orders to begin work.
d. evaluating the activities required to complete a project to find the critical path.
e. buying all the materials the organization needs.

____8. Which of the following is the first step in quality control?
a. collecting and analyzing information about the production process to pinpoint quality problems
b. assessing whether products meet quality standards
c. determining quality standards and specifications
d. inspection
e. sampling

____9. Which of the following employs specialized computer systems to actually guide and control the transformation process?
a. computer-assisted manufacturing
b. computer-integrated manufacturing
c. computer-assisted design
d. flexible manufacturing
e. robots

____10. Which of the following is the development and administration of the activities involved in transforming resources into goods and services?
a. production
b. manufacturing
c. quality control
d. operations management
e. logistics

Chapter 9 Production and Operations Management

____11.   Which of the following makes products with interchangeable parts according to agreed-to specifications?
   a.   standardization
   b.   customization
   c.   modular design
   d.   project organizations
   e.   intermittent organizations

____12.   Which of the following is NOT an input?
   a.   labor
   b.   services
   c.   materials
   d.   energy
   e.   money

____13.   When management collects and analyzes information about the production process to pinpoint quality problems, it is engaging in
   a.   inventory control.
   b.   quality control.
   c.   statistical process control.
   d.   logistics.
   e.   none of the above.

____14.   Which of the following is NOT part of logistics?
   a.   inventory control
   b.   routing
   c.   purchasing
   d.   scheduling
   e.   capacity planning

____15.   Which of the following schedules the precise quantity of materials needed to make the product?
   a.   economic order quantity model
   b.   just-in-time inventory management
   c.   material-requirements planning
   d.   statistical process control
   e.   logistics

Chapter 9 Production and Operations Management

SKILL-BUILDING QUIZ

In the "Build Your Skills" exercise of your text, you practiced identifying strengths and weaknesses related to cycle time. Build on this skill by choosing the correct answer for each of the following.

_____1. Which dimension of cycle time relates to each product being tailored to customer needs?
    a. speed
    b. connectivity
    c. interactivity
    d. customization
    e. responsiveness

_____2. Which dimension of cycle time would be most effected by the installation of computerized ordering capabilities at a fast-food restaurant?
    a. connectivity
    b. speed
    c. interactivity
    d. customization
    e. responsiveness

_____3. What is the goal of cycle time reduction?
    a. to reduce the number of hours worked per employee
    b. to reduce the production process speed
    c. to reduce costs and/or increase customer service
    d. to reduce product defects
    e. to reduce the number of revolutions involved in the production process

_____4. Which dimension of cycle time relates to the willingness to make adjustments and be flexible to help customers and to provide prompt service when a problem develops?
    a. responsiveness
    b. speed
    c. connectivity
    d. customization
    e. interactivity

Chapter 9 Production and Operations Management

ANSWERS

MATCHING QUIZ

1. c   2. d   3. b   4. a

TRUE/FALSE QUIZ

1. F	5. F	9. F	13. T	17. T
2. T	6. F	10. T	14. F	18. F
3. T	7. T	11. F	15. T	19. T
4. F	8. F	12. T	16. F	20. T

MULTIPLE-CHOICE QUIZ

1. e	4. b	7. a	10. d	13. c
2. b	5. e	8. c	11. a	14. e
3. d	6. d	9. a	12. b	15. c

SKILL-BUILDING QUIZ

1. d   2. b   3. c   4. a

Chapter 10 Motivating the Work Force

CHAPTER OUTLINE

Introduction

Nature of Human Relations

Historical Perspectives on Employee Motivation
        Classical Theory of Motivation
        The Hawthorne Studies

Theories of Employee Motivation
        Maslow's Hierarchy of Needs
        Herzberg's Two-Factor Theory
        McGregor's Theory X and Theory Y
        Theory Z
        Variations on Theory Z
        Equity Theory
        Expectancy Theory

Strategies for Motivating Employees
        Behaviour Modification
        Job Design
        Importance of Motivational Strategies

CHAPTER OBJECTIVES

After reading this chapter, you should be able to:
- Define human relations and determine why its study is important.
- Summarize early studies that laid the groundwork for understanding employee motivation.
- Compare and contrast the human-relations theories of Abraham Maslow and Frederick Herzberg.
- Investigate various theories of motivation, including theories X, Y. and Z; equity theory; and expectancy theory.
- Describe some of the strategies that managers use to motivate employees.
- Critique a business's program for motivating its sales force.

CHAPTER RECAP

NATURE OF HUMAN RELATIONS

What motivates employees to perform on the job is the focus of **human relations,** the study of the behaviour of individuals and groups in organizational settings. The field of human relations has become increasingly important as businesses strive to understand how to motivate their increasingly diverse employees to be more effective, boost workplace morale, and maximize employees' productivity and creativity. **Motivation** is an inner drive that directs behavior toward goals. A goal is the satisfaction of some need, and a need is the difference between a desired state and an actual state. Motivation explains why people behave as they do. One important aspect of human relations is **morale**--an employee's attitude toward his or her job, employer, and colleagues. High morale

Chapter 10 Motivating the Work Force

contributes to high levels of productivity and employee loyalty; low morale may cause high rates of absenteeism and turnover (when employees quit or are fired and must be replaced by new employees).

HISTORICAL PERSPECTIVES ON EMPLOYEE MOTIVATION

Throughout the twentieth century, researchers have conducted numerous studies to try to identify ways to motivate workers and increase productivity.

Time and motion studies conducted by Frederick W. Taylor and by Frank and Lillian Gilbreth at the turn of the century analyzed how workers perform specific work tasks in an effort to improve the employees' productivity. These efforts led to the application of scientific management, which focused on improving work methods, tools, and performance standards. According to the **Classical theory of motivation**, money is the sole motivator for workers. To improve productivity, Taylor thought that managers should break each job down into its component tasks (specialization), determine the best way to perform each task, and specify the output to be achieved by a worker performing the task. Taylor also believed that incentives motivate employees to be more productive. We can still see Taylor's ideas in practice today in the use of mathematical models, statistics, and incentives. Taylor and most early twentieth-century managers generally believed that money and job security were the primary motivators of employees.

In the Hawthorne studies, Elton Mayo and a team of researchers tried to determine what physical conditions in the workplace, such as light and noise levels stimulate employees to be most productive. Their studies revealed that social and psychological factors significantly affect productivity and morale and that managers who understand employees' needs, beliefs, and expectations are most successful in motivating them. The Hawthorne studies marked the beginning of a concern for human relations in the workplace.

THEORIES OF EMPLOYEE MOTIVATION

The research of Taylor, Mayo, and others led to the development of a number of theories that attempt to describe what motivates employees to perform. Among these are Maslow's hierarchy; Herzberg's two-factor theory; and the X, Y. Z. equity, and expectancy theories.

Abraham Maslow theorized that humans have five basic needs: physiological, security, social, esteem, and self-actualization. **Maslow's hierarchy** shows the order in which people strive to satisfy these needs. **Physiological needs,** the most basic and first needs to be satisfied, are the essentials for living-- water, food, shelter, and clothing. Once physiological needs have been met, people concentrate on **security needs,** the need to protect oneself from physical and economic harm. Next, people attempt to satisfy their **social needs,** the need for love, companionship, and friendship--the desire for acceptance by others. When social needs have been fulfilled, people try to satisfy **esteem needs,** which relate to self-respect and respect from others. Only after all the other needs have been satisfied do people strive for **self-actualization needs,** that is, being the best that one can be. Maslow's theory maintains that the more basic needs at the bottom of the hierarchy must be satisfied before higher-level goals are pursued. It also suggests that employees will be motivated to contribute to organizational goals only if they are able first to satisfy their physiological, security, and social needs through their work.

Psychologist Frederick Herzberg proposed a theory of motivation that focuses on the job and on the environment where work is done. **Hygiene factors**, which relate to the work setting, not to the content

Chapter 10 Motivating the Work Force

of the work, include adequate wages, comfortable and safe working conditions, fair company policies, and job security. These factors do not necessarily motivate employees to excel, but their absence may be a source of dissatisfaction for employees. They are similar to Maslow's physiological and security needs. **Motivational factors;** which relate to the content of the work itself, include achievement, recognition, involvement, responsibility, and advancement. Herzberg's motivational factors and Maslow's esteem and self-actualization needs are similar. Herzberg's theory implies that to improve productivity, management should try to satisfy workers' higher-level needs (motivational factors) by providing opportunities for achievement, involvement, and advancement and by recognizing good performance.

Douglas McGregor related Maslow's ideas about personal needs to management when he developed two contrasting views of management. Managers adopting **Theory X** assume that workers generally dislike work and must be forced to do their jobs. Theory X managers maintain tight control over workers, provide almost constant supervision, try to motivate through fear, make decisions in an autocratic fashion, and do not take into account employees' needs for companionship, esteem, and personal growth. Managers subscribing to the **Theory Y** view assume that workers like to work and that under proper conditions employees will seek out responsibility in an attempt to satisfy their social, esteem, and self-actualization needs. Theory Y managers maintain less control and supervision than do Theory X managers, do not use fear as a motivator, and are more democratic in decision making.

Theory Z, developed by William Ouchi, is a management philosophy that stresses employee participation in all aspects of company decision making. This theory incorporates many elements associated with the Japanese approach to management, such as trust and intimacy, but Japanese ideas have been adapted for use in North America. In a Theory Z organization, managers and workers share responsibilities; the management style is participative; and employment is long-term and often lifelong.

Theory Z has been adapted and modified for use in a number of organizations. One adaptation involves workers in decisions through **quality circles,** which are small groups, usually having five to eight members who discuss ways to reduce waste, eliminate problems, and improve quality, communication, and work satisfaction. Even more involved are programs known by such terms as *participative management, employee involvement,* or *self-directed work teams,* which strive to give employees more control over their jobs while making them more responsible for the outcome of their efforts.

According to **equity theory,** how much people are willing to contribute to an organization depends on their assessment of the fairness, or equity, of the rewards they will receive in exchange. Each worker regularly develops a personal input-output ratio by taking stock of his or her contribution (inputs) to the organization in time, effort, skills, and experience and assessing the rewards (outputs) offered by the organization in pay, benefits, recognition, and promotions. The worker compares his or her ratio to the input-output ratio of some other person--a coworker, a friend working in another organization, or an "average" of several people working in the organization. If the two ratios are close, the individual will feel that he or she is being treated equitably. This theory implies that managers should try to avoid equity problems by ensuring that rewards are distributed on the basis of performance and that all employees clearly understand the basis for their pay and benefits.

Victor Vroom described **expectancy theory,** which states that motivation depends not only on how much a person wants something, but on the person's perception of how likely he or she is to get it.

Chapter 10 Motivating the Work Force

STRATEGIES FOR MOTIVATING EMPLOYEES

Behaviour modification, developed by B. F. Skinner, involves changing behaviour and encouraging appropriate actions by relating the consequences of behaviour to the behaviour Itself. Behaviour that is rewarded will tend to be repeated; behaviour that is punished will tend to be eliminated. Punishing behaviour may provide quick results, but may lead to undesirable long-term side effects. Rewarding appropriate behaviour is generally more effective in modifying behaviour in the long run.

There are several strategies that managers may use to design jobs to promote employee motivation. **Job rotation** allows employees to move from one job to another to relieve boredom associated with specialization. Eventually, however, employees will become bored with all the tasks in the cycle. **Job enlargement** adds more tasks to a job instead of treating each task as a separate job. Its rationale is that jobs become more satisfying as the number of tasks performed increases. **Job enrichment** incorporates motivational factors, such as opportunity for achievement, recognition, responsibility, and advancement into a job. This strategy not only gives a worker more tasks but also more control and authority over the job

Flexible scheduling strategies help managers deal with the problems of poor motivation and high absenteeism, as well as address the needs of a diverse work force. **Flextime** allows employees to choose their starting and ending work times as long as they are at work during a specified core time and work the specified number of hours. The **compressed work week** is a four-day (or shorter) period in which employees work 40 hours. **Job sharing** occurs when two people do one job. Other flexible scheduling strategies gaining in popularity are allowing full-time workers to work part time and allowing workers to work at home part time. Such flexible work schedules give more options to employees who are trying to juggle work and family responsibilities.

Management by objectives (MBO) is a process in which a manager and a subordinate conferring together set and agree to goals for the subordinate to achieve. Managers periodically conduct performance reviews to see how well the employee is progressing toward achievement of the goals. At the end of the specified time, the employee is rewarded on the basis of how close he or she came to achieving the goals. The rationale behind MBO is that employees who are involved in the goal-setting process will be highly motivated to perform.

Motivation is not only a tool that managers can use to foster employee loyalty and boost productivity, but also a process that affects all the relationships within an organization and influences many areas such as pay, promotion, job design, training opportunities, and reporting relationships.

Chapter 10 Motivating the Work Force

ENHANCEMENT EXERCISES

Watching people react to various motivational and managerial techniques can be highly informative and interesting to study. Obtain several puzzles of 100 pieces or more. Break the class into an equal number of groups and provide each group a puzzle. Have the groups select a manager and call that manager outside the group. Each manager should be assigned a different motivational technique from the text that he/she must use in organizing and leading the construction of the puzzle. Afterward, reflect on which group finished first and which finished last. What are the groups' comments on the different motivational and managerial styles?

MATCHING QUIZ

Match the following statements with the correct key term.

a. Theory X
b. Theory Y
c. Theory Z
d. equity theory
e. expectancy theory

_____1.   This theory suggests that how much people are willing to contribute to an organization depends on their assessment of the fairness of the rewards they will receive in exchange.

_____2.   This theory assumes that workers generally dislike work and must be forced to do their jobs.

_____3.   This theory stresses employee participation in all aspects of company decision making.

_____4.   This theory suggests that motivation depends not only on how much a person wants something, but on his or her perception of how likely he or she is to get it.

_____5.   This theory assumes that workers like to work and that under proper conditions, employees will seek out responsibility in an attempt to satisfy their social, esteem, and self-actualization needs.

TRUE/FALSE QUIZ

Indicate whether each of the following statements is true or false.

_____1.   Security needs relate to protecting yourself from physical and economic harm.

_____2.   Theory Z is the Japanese style of management.

_____3.   Job enrichment enhances a worker's feeling of responsibility and provides opportunities for growth and advancement.

Chapter 10 Motivating the Work Force

_____4.   Herzberg's hygiene factors and Maslow's esteem and self-actualization needs are similar.

_____5.   A need is an inner state directing behavior toward goals.

_____6.   Once people have satisfied their esteem needs, they strive for security needs.

_____7.   Equity theory implies that managers should ensure that rewards are distributed on the basis of performance and that all employees clearly understand the basis for their pay and benefits.

_____8.   Under flextime, a person might go to work at 6:00 A.M. and leave at 2:00 P.M. in order to attend afternoon classes.

_____9.   Low morale may be a cause of high rates of absenteeism.

_____10.   Motivational factors include high wages, comfortable working conditions, and job security.

_____11.   According to expectancy theory, a person who does not believe that he or she can get a private office will be motivated to work hard in order to get one anyway.

_____12.   Flexible scheduling strategies, because they have been ineffective in motivating employees, are declining in use.

_____13.   Victor Vroom is called "the father of scientific management."

_____14.   Theory Y managers are democratic leaders.

_____15.   If a person has his or her pay docked for tardiness, he or she will probably make a greater effort to arrive at work on time in the future.

_____16.   Management by objectives allows an organization to constantly emphasize what must be done in order to achieve organizational objectives.

_____17.   Theory X managers help their employees achieve all five of Maslow's hierarchy of needs.

_____18.   In the Hawthorne studies, employee productivity increased regardless of physical conditions in the work environment.

_____19.   Job rotation is more successful in increasing job satisfaction than is job enlargement.

_____20.   Elton Mayo discovered the Hawthorne effect.

Chapter 10 Motivating the Work Force

MULTIPLE-CHOICE QUIZ

Choose the correct answer for each of the following questions.

_____1.   Which of the following assumes that workers must be coerced, controlled, and even threatened to get them to work toward organizational objectives?
   a.   equity theory
   b.   Theory X
   c.   Theory Y
   d.   Theory Z
   e.   expectancy theory

_____2.   A person who believes that his or her input-output ratio is lower than that of some "comparison other" might take which of the following actions?
   a.   recommend that the "comparison other" receive a raise
   b.   ask for a raise
   c.   offer to take a cut in pay
   d.   work longer hours
   e.   none of the above

_____3.   Which of the following is NOT a part of the Classical theory of motivation?
   a.   Rotate tasks.
   b.   Break jobs down into component tasks.
   c.   Specify the output to be achieved by a worker performing the task.
   d.   Determine the best way to perform a task.
   e.   Link workers' pay directly to their output.

_____4.   Which of the following is the difference between a desired state and an actual state?
   a.   motivation
   b.   goal
   c.   maintenance
   d.   morale
   e.   need

_____5.   Which of the following assumes that workers will seek out responsibility and exercise self-direction and self-control?
   a.   expectancy theory
   b.   Theory X
   c.   Theory Y
   d.   Theory Z
   e.   behaviour modification theory

Chapter 10 Motivating the Work Force

_____6.   Which of the following job-design strategies involves incorporating motivational factors into a job?
    a. job rotation
    b. job enlargement
    c. job enrichment
    d. flextime
    e. job sharing

_____7.   Which of the following is NOT one of Maslow's hierarchy of needs?
    a. physiological needs
    b. esteem needs
    c. social needs
    d. self-actualization needs
    e. maintenance needs

_____8.   Which of the following assumes that workers can participate in decision making and management?
    a. behavioural theory
    b. Theory X
    c. Theory Y
    d. Theory Z
    e. expectancy theory

_____9.   Which of the following job-design strategies allows employees to move from job to job?
    a. job rotation
    b. job enlargement
    c. job enrichment
    d. flextime
    e. job sharing

_____10.   Who developed the concept of behaviour modification?
    a. Frederick Herzberg
    b. Abraham Maslow
    c. Victor Vroom
    d. B. F. Skinner
    e. Elton Mayo

_____11.   Who suggested the expectancy theory?
    a. Victor Vroom
    b. William Ouchi
    c. Abraham Maslow
    d. B. F. Skinner
    e. Frederick Taylor

Chapter 10 Motivating the Work Force

_____12.   Which of the following allows employees to take a three-day weekend?
   a.   job enlargement
   b.   compressed work week
   c.   job sharing
   d.   flextime
   e.   a really nice boss

_____13.   According to Herzberg, which of the following is most likely to motivate workers to work harder?
   a.   fair company policies
   b.   wages
   c.   job security
   d.   comfortable working environment
   e.   recognition

_____14.   Which of the following states that motivation depends not only on how much a person wants something but also on the person's perception of how likely he or she is to get it?
   a.   Maslow's hierarchy
   b.   classical theory of motivation
   c.   behaviour modification
   d.   expectancy theory
   e.   equity theory

_____15.   Which of the following is NOT a part of management by objectives?
   a.   Subordinates negotiate goals with their superiors.
   b.   Subordinates are rewarded according to how close they came to achieving their goals.
   c.   Subordinates are rewarded for achieving organizational objectives.
   d.   Managers conduct performance reviews to see how subordinates are progressing toward objectives.
   e.   All of the above are part of MBO.

Chapter 10 Motivating the Work Force

SKILL-BUILDING QUIZ

In the "Build Your Skills" exercise, you looked at how play can motivate. Many companies are trying to incorporate characteristics of play into their practices in an effort to improve employee satisfaction, morale, and productivity, and to reduce turnover. Examples include employee softball/volleyball/basketball teams (sometimes competing in citywide leagues against other companies' teams), company picnics, hike and bike trails on company grounds for employees to use during lunch and breaks, casual dress days, talent shows, and more. With this in mind, choose the best answer for each of the following.

____1.   Competitive sports events, whether pitting intercompany teams against each other or against other companies' teams, can help foster morale. Which of Maslow's needs do such competitions satisfy?
   a.   physiological and security
   b.   security and social
   c.   social and esteem
   d.   esteem and self-actualization
   e.   security and esteem

____2.   An intercompany talent show can provide lots of laughs, bring previously hidden creative talent to light, and help put supervisors and subordinates on a temporarily equal footing. The applause and recognition talent show participants receive can also
   a.   fulfill equity needs.
   b.   fulfill security needs.
   c.   be a maintenance factor.
   d.   be a motivational factor.
   e.   all of the above

____3.   Characteristics of play include the opportunity to express yourself and to use your unique talents. Which of Maslow's needs do these satisfy?
   a.   esteem and self-actualization
   b.   social and esteem
   c.   security and social
   d.   physiological and security
   e.   maintenance

Chapter 10 Motivating the Work Force

ANSWERS

MATCHING QUIZ

1. d   2. a   3. c   4. e   5. b

TRUE/FALSE QUIZ

1. T	5. F	9. T	13. F	17. F
2. F	6. F	10. F	14. T	18. T
3. T	7. T	11. F	15. T	19. F
4. F	8. T	12. F	16. T	20. T

MULTIPLE-CHOICE QUIZ

1. b	4. e	7. e	10. d	13. e
2. b	5. c	8. d	11. a	14. d
3. a	6. c	9. a	12. b	15. c

SKILL-BUILDING QUIZ

1. c   2. d   3. a

Chapter 11 Managing Human Resources

CHAPTER OUTLINE

Introduction

The Nature of Human Resources Management

Planning for Human Resources Needs

Recruiting and Selecting New Employees
       Recruiting
       Selection
       Legal Issues in Recruiting and Selecting
       Affirmative Action

Developing the Work Force
       Training and Development
       Assessing Performance
       Turnover

Compensating the Work Force
       Financial Compensation
       Benefits

Managing Unionized Employees
       Collective Bargaining
       Resolving Disputes

The Importance of Work-Force Diversity
       The Characteristics of Diversity
       Why is Diversity Important?
       The Benefits of Work-Force Diversity
       Affirmative Action

CHAPTER OBJECTIVES

After reading this chapter, you should be able to:
- Define human resources management and explain its significance.
- Summarize the processes of recruiting and selecting human resources for a company.
- Discuss how workers are trained and their performance appraised.
- Identify the types of turnover companies may experience, and explain why turnover is an important issue.
- Specify the various ways a worker may be compensated.
- Discuss some of the issues associated with unionized employees, including collective bargaining and dispute resolution.
- Describe the importance of diversity in the work force.
- Assess an organization's efforts to reduce its work-force size and manage the resulting effects.

Chapter 11 Managing Human Resources

INTRODUCTION

Managing the quantity (through hiring and firing) and quality (through training, compensating, and so on) of employees is an important business function.

THE NATURE OF HUMAN RESOURCES MANAGEMENT

Previously, human resources was defined as labour, the physical and mental abilities that people use to produce goods and services. **Human resources management (HRM)** refers to all the activities involved in determining an organization's human resources needs as well as acquiring, training, and compensating people to fill those needs. Human resource managers are concerned with maximizing the satisfaction of employees and motivating them to meet organizational objectives productively. HRM has increased in importance over the last few decades, in part because managers have developed a better understanding of human relations through the work of Maslow, Herzberg, and others. Moreover, the nature of the human resources themselves is changing.

PLANNING FOR HUMAN RESOURCES NEEDS

When planning and developing strategies for reaching the organization's objectives, a company must consider whether it will have the human resources necessary to carry out its plans. After determining how many employees and what skills are needed to satisfy the overall plans, human resources managers ascertain how many employees the company currently has and how many will be retiring or otherwise leaving the organization during the planning period. The human resources manager then forecasts how many more employees the company will need to hire and what qualifications they must have. HRM planning also requires forecasting the supply of people in the work force who will have the necessary qualifications to meet the organization's future needs. Next, the human resources manager develops a strategy for satisfying the organization's human resources needs.

Human resources managers analyze the jobs within the firm so that they can match the human resources to the available jobs. **Job analysis** determines, through observation and study, pertinent information about a job--the specific tasks that comprise the job; the knowledge, skills, and abilities necessary to perform the job; and the environment in which the job will be performed. A **job description** is a formal, written explanation of a specific job and usually includes job title, tasks to be performed, relationship with other jobs, physical and mental skills required, duties, responsibilities, and working conditions. A **job specification** describes the qualifications necessary for a specific job in terms of education, experience, personal characteristics, and physical characteristics. These analyses help human resources managers develop recruiting materials such as newspaper advertisements.

RECRUITING AND SELECTING NEW EMPLOYEES

Recruiting means forming a pool of qualified applicants from which management can select employees. Internal sources of applicants include the organization's current employees. External sources consist of advertisements in newspapers and professional journals, employment agencies, colleges, vocational schools, recommendations from current employees, and unsolicited applications.

Chapter 11 Managing Human Resources

Selection is the process of collecting information about applicants and using that information to decide which ones to hire. It includes the application, testing interviewing, and reference checking. If a firm finds the "right" employees through this process, it will not have to spend as much money later in recruiting, selecting, and training replacement employees. In the first stage of the process, the applicant fills out an application form and perhaps has a brief interview. The goal is to get acquainted with the applicants and to weed out those who are obviously not qualified for the job. The next stage involves interviewing applicants to obtain detailed information about the their experience and skills, reasons for changing jobs, attitudes toward the job, and an idea of whether they would fit in with the company The third step involves testing applicants through ability, performance, aptitude, IQ, physical, and other tests to assess an applicant's potential and skills. Finally before making a job offer, the company should always check applicants' references.

Legal constraints and regulations are present in almost every phase of the recruitment and selection process, and violations of these regulations can result in lawsuits and fines. Each province and territory, as well as the federal government, have Human Rights laws governing individual rights and freedoms from discrimination based on race, religion, sexual orientation, age, gender, etc. These laws extend to the work place in both the treatment of employees and the hiring procedures. The federal government enacted in 1987 the Employment Equity Act that governs the hiring practices of those organizations under its jurisdiction such as airlines and banks. The act requires that employers with over 100 employees develop annual plans to include "persons in a designated group achieve a degree of representation commensurate with their representation in the Canadian workforce and their ability to meet reasonable occupational requirements."

Employment Equity Programs have been developed by employers to undo past discrimination or to ensure equal employment opportunities in the future. Although no province at this time requires that organizations under their jurisdiction be required to fulfill these same equity programs though many public and private organizations do so voluntarily.

DEVELOPING THE WORK FORCE

After applicants have been offered jobs, they must be formally introduced to the organization and trained. **Orientation** familiarizes newly hired employees with coworkers, company procedures, and the physical properties of the company. It also socializes new employees into the ethics and culture of the new company.

New employees must undergo **training** to learn how to do their specific job tasks. On-the-job training allows workers to learn by actually performing the tasks of the job, while classroom training teaches employees with lectures, conferences, videotapes, case studies, and web-based training used in a classroom. **Development** is training that augments the skills and knowledge of managers and professionals. Training and development are also used to improve the skills of employees in their present positions and to prepare them for increased responsibility and job promotions.

Assessing an employee's performance--strengths and weaknesses on the job--gives employees feedback on how they are doing and what they need to do to improve their performance; provides a basis for determining how to compensate and reward employees; and generates information about the quality of the firm's selection, training, and development activities. Performance appraisals may be objective or subjective. Objective assessments are quantifiable. Subjective appraisals relate the employee's performance to some standard. Performance appraisals are also used to determine whether an employee should be promoted, transferred, or terminated from the organization.

A **promotion** is an advancement to a higher-level job with increased authority, responsibility, and pay. A **transfer** is a move to another job within the company at essentially the same level and wage. **Separations** occur when employees resign, retire, are terminated, or are laid off. Employees may be terminated or fired for poor performance violation of work rules, absenteeism, and so on. Recent legislation and court decisions now require that companies fire employees fairly, for just cause only. A well-organized human resources department strives to minimize losses due to separations and transfers because recruiting and training new employees is very expensive. A high turnover rate in a company may signal problems with the selection or training process or with the compensation program.

COMPENSATING THE WORK FORCE

Designing a fair compensation plan is an important task because pay and benefits represent a substantial portion of an organization's expenses. Compensation for a specific job is typically determined through a **wage/salary survey**, which tells the company how much compensation comparable firms are paying for specific jobs that the firms have in common. Compensation for individuals within a specific job category depends on the compensation for that job and the individual's productivity.

Wages are financial rewards based on the number of hours an employee works or the level of output achieved. Time wages, based on the number of hours worked, are most appropriate when employees are continually interrupted and when quality is more important than quantity. Wages may also be based on an incentive system, using either piece wages or commissions. Piece wages are based on the level of output achieved and are most appropriate when work is standardized and when the output of each employee can be accurately measured. The other incentive system, commission, pays a fixed amount or a percentage of the employee's sales. A **salary** is a financial reward calculated on a weekly, monthly, or annual basis. In addition to the basic wages or salaries paid to employees, a company may offer **bonuses** for exceptional performance as an incentive to increase productivity further. Another form of compensation is **profit-sharing**, which distributes a percentage of company profits to the employees whose work helped to generate those profits. Some profit-sharing plans distribute shares of company stock to employees through employee stock ownership plans (ESOPs).

Benefits are nonfinancial forms of compensation provided to employees, such as pension plans for retirement; health, disability, and life insurance; holidays and paid days off for vacation or illness; credit union membership; health programs; child care; elder care; assistance with adoption; and more. Benefits increase employee security and, to a certain extent, morale and motivation. A benefit increasingly offered is the employee assistance program (EAP), which usually provides counseling for and assistance with employees' personal problems that might hurt their job performance if not addressed. Companies try to provide the benefits they believe their employees want, but diverse people may want different things.

MANAGING UNIONIZED EMPLOYEES

Employees who are dissatisfied with their working conditions or compensation negotiate with management to bring about change. Dealing with management on an individual basis is not always effective, however, so employees may organize themselves into **labour unions** to deal with employers and to achieve better pay, hours, and working conditions. Union growth has

Chapter 11 Managing Human Resources

slowed in recent years because most blue-collar workers have already been organized; factories have become automated and need fewer blue-collar workers; the economy has become more service-oriented, which requires fewer blue-collar workers; and job enrichment programs and participative management have blurred the line between management and workers. Nonetheless, labour unions have been successful in organizing blue-collar manufacturing, government, and health-care workers, as well as smaller percentages of employees in other industries. Consequently, significant aspects of HRM, particularly compensation, are dictated to a large degree by union contract at many companies.

Collective bargaining is the negotiation process through which management and unions reach an agreement about compensation, working hours, and working conditions for the bargaining unit. The objective of negotiations is to reach agreement about a **labour contract**, the formal, written document that spells out the relationship between the union and management for a specified period of time, usually two or three years. In collective bargaining, each side tries to negotiate an agreement that meets its demands; compromise is frequently necessary. Many labour contracts contain a cost-of-living escalator clause (COLA), which calls for automatic wage increases during periods of inflation but, during tough economic times, unions may be forced to accept givebacks--wage and benefit concessions made to employers to help them remain competitive and continue to provide jobs for union workers.

Most labour disputes are handled through collective bargaining or grievance procedures. When these processes break down, however, either side may resort to more drastic measures to achieve its objectives. Labour tactics include **picketing**, a public protest against management practices with union members marching (often waving antimanagement signs and placards) at the employer's plant; **strikes**, employee walkouts; and **boycotts**, when union members are asked not to do business with the boycotted organization. Management's version of a strike is the **lockout**; the work site is actually closed so that employees cannot go to work. Management may also hire **strikebreakers**, or "scabs," to replace striking employees.

Sometimes, even after lengthy negotiations, strikes, and lockouts, management and labour still cannot resolve a contract dispute. In such cases, outside intervention may be necessary. **Conciliation** brings in a neutral third party to keep labour and management talking. **Mediation** brings in a neutral third party to suggest or propose a solution to the problem. **Arbitration** brings in a neutral third party to settle the dispute; the arbitrator's solution is legally binding and enforceable. Management and labour may submit to compulsory arbitration, in which an outside party (usually the federal government) requests arbitration as a means of eliminating a prolonged strike that threatens to disrupt the economy.

THE IMPORTANCE OF WORK-FORCE DIVERSITY

The participation of different ages, genders, races, ethnicities, nationalities, and abilities in the workplace is known as **diversity**. Differences can be divided into primary and secondary characteristics of diversity to enhance our understanding. The Canadian work force is becoming increasingly diverse.

Women, blacks, Hispanics, and other minorities, and the disabled have traditionally faced discrimination. Consequently, more companies are trying to improve HRM programs to recruit, develop, and retain more diverse employees to better serve their diverse customers. Effectively managing diversity in the work force involves cultivating and valuing its benefits and minimizing its problems.

Chapter 11 Managing Human Resources

Fostering and valuing work-force diversity has numerous benefits: more productive use of a company's human resources; reduced conflict among employees; more productive working relationships among diverse employees; increased commitment to and sharing of organizational goals among employees at all organizational levels increased innovation and creativity as diverse employees bring new, unique perspectives to decision-making and problem-solving tasks; and increased ability to serve the needs of an increasingly diverse customer base. Companies that do not value their diverse employees are likely to experience greater conflict, as well as prejudice and discrimination. A discriminatory atmosphere can not only harm productivity and raise turnover, but it may also subject a firm to costly lawsuits and negative publicity.

Astute businesses recognize that they need to modify their HRM programs (recruiting, selecting, compensating, benefits, etc.) to target the needs of *all* their diverse employees as well as those of the firm itself. As workforce diversity becomes a valued organizational asset, companies spend less time managing conflict and more time accomplishing tasks and satisfying customers.

ENHANCEMENT EXERCISES

1. The following situation is a union negotiations role-play. The class should be broken into groups and designated as either company representatives or union representatives. A time limit is given of 15 to 30 minutes and students are instructed to either reach a settlement or declare a strike in that time. *Hint:* One of the best ways to improve the intensity of the negotiations is to offer a prize to the team that arrive at the best settlement for their respective side.

Situation:

Manda Inc. is a growing private company specializing in Internet data base marketing/mining and software construction. The company was founded by Michael Joseph in 1993 and after years of struggling, has finally started to show a nice profit. The company, up until one year ago, had 44 employees all working on a contract basis. Michael moved to sign all employees to regular contracts with a small pension plan including stock options, but no other benefits. Last month the company workers formed a union and contract negotiations have started.

The company's annual average salary is 10% better then the industry average (6 companies in average - no skew in place) while the stock options and pension plans are slightly lower. In regards to health, dental, life and disability, the company ranks last in industry averages. Michael realizes he will have to pay some benefits in the contract, but after years of struggling and setting the pay above the industry average, he doesn't feel obliged to pay much. The employees see other benefit plans (including plans for full family coverage) in place and believe that Michael should introduce a package above the industry average of $320,000 for a similar sized workforce.

Notes:
This company ranks third in sales and profit among six competitors. Salary problems have been solved but a strike looms around the benefits package. Business analysts are predicting the company will move up to second in profits and sales shortly. The industry is growing.

The company is located in a small town away from competitors, so many employees want the lifestyle they are living thus other employment options are not great - but look like they may be improving in the near future.

Keys - The key to success in this role-play is the ability of people to play a role and pretend the situation actually exists. Michael and his management team are considered cheap and insensitive.

The union claims to be just as tough but fair. But both sides understand that no one wins if a strike is declared, but neither wants to give away too much.

Dental:
a) partial coverage - $40,000
b) full coverage - $80,000
c) family coverage - $120,000

Medical:
a) partial - $45,000
b) full - $90,000
c) partial family - $110,000
d) full family - $130,000

Life Insurance:
a) partial payment - $35,000
b) full payment - $60,000
c) partial spousal plan - $75,000
d) full spousal plan - $90,000

Disability:
   a) 25% - $30,000
   b) 50% - $60,000
   c) 75% - $90,000
   d) 100% - $120,000

MATCHING QUIZ

Match the following statements with the correct key term.
a. job analysis
b. job description
c. job specification
d. conciliation
e. mediation
f. arbitration

_____1.   A description of the qualifications necessary for a specific job, in terms of education, experience, personal characteristics, and physical characteristics.

_____2.   A dispute-resolution method that brings in a neutral third party to settle the dispute; the arbitrator's solution is legally binding and enforceable.

_____3.   A formal, written explanation of a specific job, which usually includes job title, tasks to be performed, relationship with other jobs, physical and mental skills required, duties, responsibilities, and working conditions.

_____4.   A dispute-resolution method that brings in a neutral third party to keep labour and management talking.

_____5.   The process of determining, through observation and study, pertinent information

Chapter 11 Managing Human Resources

about a job--the specific tasks that comprise the job; the knowledge, skills, and abilities necessary to perform the job; and the environment in which the job will be performed.

_____6.   A dispute-resolution method that brings in a neutral third party to suggest or propose a solution to the problem.

TRUE/FALSE QUIZ

Indicate whether each of the following statements is true or false.

_____1.   Applications allow an organization to weed out those job seekers who are unacceptable for a particular job.

_____2.   Classroom training teaches workers by having them perform the tasks of the job.

_____3.   Compensation for a particular job is usually determined through a job evaluation.

_____4.   Union growth has slowed in recent years.

_____5.   Human resources managers are concerned with maximizing the satisfaction of employees and motivating them to meet organizational objectives productively.

_____6.   The Equal Pay Act prohibits discrimination in employment.

_____7.   Diversity characteristics can be divided into two groups: primary and secondary.

_____8.   Piece wages are an incentive system.

_____9.   Human resources management has increased in importance both because of the work of Maslow and others and the changing nature of the human resources themselves.

_____10.   Recruiting is the process of collecting information about applicants and using that information to decide which ones to hire.

_____11.   One of the purposes of performance appraisal is providing a basis for determining how to compensate and reward employees.

_____12.   Bonuses are nonfinancial forms of compensation provided to employees.

_____13.   A job analysis is a formal, written description of the qualifications necessary for a specific job.

_____14.   The actual number of worker-days lost to strikes is less than the amount lost to the common cold.

_____15.   A resignation occurs when an organization fires an employee.

_____16.   Affirmative action has brought about equality among women and minorities in the work force.

Chapter 11 Managing Human Resources

_____17.   Headhunters are an internal source for recruiting new employees.

_____18.   Boycotts are a management tactic for resolving disputes.

_____19.   Organizations should try to minimize separations and transfers to reduce costs associated with recruiting and training new employees.

_____20.   Examples of benefits include insurance, vacation and sick pay, credit unions, and health programs.

MULTIPLE-CHOICE QUIZ

Choose the correct answer for each of the following questions.

_____1.   Which of the following selection stages assesses an applicant's potential for a certain kind of work?
   a.   application
   b.   testing
   c.   interview
   d.   reference checking
   e.   orientation

_____2.   Which of the following is NOT a separation?
   a.   transfer
   b.   termination
   c.   layoff
   d.   retirement
   e.   resignation

_____3.   Canada's affirmative action program is referred to as _____.
   a.   Employment Equity Program
   b.   Human Rights
   c.   Equal Pay Act
   d.   Equal Employment Opportunity Act
   e.   Fair Play Act

_____4.   Which of the following is NOT a function of human resources management?
   a.   planning
   b.   recruiting and selection
   c.   compensation
   d.   training and development
   e.   directing

_____5.   Which of the following is NOT a reason for the decline in union growth?
   a.   Companies are using job-enrichment programs and participative management to boost competitiveness.
   b.   Canada has become a service economy with fewer blue-collar workers.

    c.   Union dues are too high.
    d.   Automated factories need fewer blue-collar workers.
    e.   Most blue-collar workers have already been organized.

_____6.   Which of the following is an incentive compensation system?
    a.   time wage
    b.   salary
    c.   bonus
    d.   commission
    e.   raise

_____7.   Which of the following familiarizes newly hired employees with fellow workers, company procedures, and the physical properties of the company?
    a.   testing
    b.   training
    c.   recruiting
    d.   selection
    e.   orientation

_____8.   When companies downsize and lay off employees, which of the following occurs?
    a.   resignation
    b.   termination
    c.   transfer
    d.   separation
    e.   promotion

_____9.   Which of the following is an advantage of using time wages?
    a.   They increase productivity.
    b.   They allow work to be standardized.
    c.   Employees are constantly interrupted.
    d.   Each employee's output is easily measured.
    e.   They are easily calculated.

_____10.   Which of the following is a formal, written explanation of a specific job?
    a.   job analysis
    b.   job description
    c.   job specification
    d.   job summary
    e.   none of the above

_____11.   Which of the following is not a benefit of fostering and valuing work-force diversity?
    a.   increased innovation and creativity
    b.   more productive relationships among employees
    c.   increased conflict and prejudice
    d.   increased commitment to and sharing of goals among employees
    e.   more effective use of human resources

_____12.   Which of the following is the most effective weapon labour has in disputes with management?
   a.   strikebreakers
   b.   lockouts
   c.   pickets
   d.   strikes
   e.   boycotts

_____13.   Which of the following is an internal recruiting source for an organization?
   a.   the company newsletter
   b.   *The Globe and Mail Career Section*
   c.   colleges
   d.   employee referrals
   e.   unsolicited applications

_____14.   Employee stock ownership plans are an example of
   a.   benefits.
   b.   profit sharing.
   c.   bonuses.
   d.   salaries.
   e.   wages.

_____15.   Which of the following allows an organization to obtain in-depth information about a job seeker?
   a.   application
   b.   testing
   c.   interview
   d.   reference checking
   e.   orientation

Chapter 11 Managing Human Resources

SKILL-BUILDING QUIZ

Throughout this text, you have read that the North American work force is very diverse and becoming increasingly more so. One training tool that companies such as Herman Miller McDonald's Corporation, Miami Herald Publishing, and Philip Morris Corporation are using to challenge their employees to handle encounters with people different from themselves is the board game DIVERSOPHY®--*Understanding the Human Race.* In DIVERSOPHY® players take turns rolling dice and moving game pieces around a multicolored board that has a pattern resembling a racetrack. Colored squares along the paths correspond to colored cards. When landing on these squares, players read a corresponding card and follow directions. This game addresses such broad diversity issues as race, gender, age, sexual orientation, and physical abilities by providing four types of challenges.[1]

- The green *diversi*Smarts™ cards develop your knowledge and awareness of other people.
- The yellow *diversi*Choice™ cards put you in everyday work situations and help you learn how to choose appropriate behaviors.
- The blue *diversi*Share™ cards provide a forum to dialogue and share personal background and experiences.
- The red *diversi*Risk™ cards allow you to experience situations of diversity.

In the "Build Your Skills" exercise, you considered diversity issues. Build on those skills by completing the following exercise, which will give you a chance to sample four of the 60 cards available in the yellow *diversi*Choice™ category. Read each situation described, examine the choices, and select the best way to deal with each situation. After completing all four questions, compare your answers with those provided on the back of the *diversi*Choice™ cards, as shown at the end of this chapter.

_____ 1. You own a small, growing high-tech assembly operation and employ workers from Latin and Middle Eastern backgrounds. You feel continually under pressure to find jobs for both their near and distant relatives. You should
   a.   explain how the legal and professional restraints prevent you from doing favors.
   b.   suggest the relatives apply for work opportunities both in your organization and elsewhere.
   c.   discourage them by refusing to listen or by changing the subject.

---

1. All materials related to DIVERSOPHY® are from ©1992 MULTUS Inc., 46 Treetop Lane, Suite 200, San Mateo, CA 94402 (415) 342-2040. Note, MULTUS has also introduced two additional sets of 180 cards each. One set is on gender, sexual harassment, and sexual orientation; the other is on global negotiation.

_____2.   You are a white male manager mentoring a minority individual. Your mentee has made a blunder that has caused your boss to come down rather hard on you. As a result, you
   a. tell your mentee exactly what has happened and what you expect him or her to do the next time.
   b. avoid upsetting your mentee by taking the heat yourself but resolving to supervise him or her more carefully in the future.
   c. remove the mentee from situations in which he or she is likely to get into similar problems with upper management.

_____3.   The people in your organization are all under 30. You like this young image and feel it sells your product.
   a. You are justified in not hiring older people because they may not fit in.
   b. You may want to hire older people for inside work to create a balance in your staff.
   c. You should disregard these considerations and base your hiring solely on objective, job-related criteria, without respect to age.

_____4.   You find it hard to understand an employee whose accent is very different from yours. You have asked this person to repeat twice. What should you do next?
   a. Apologize for not understanding and politely ask him or her to repeat again, perhaps in other words.
   b. Look for a translator and ask him or her to speak in his or her native language.
   c. Get on with the conversation; the context will clarify what you have not understood.

ANSWERS

MATCHING QUIZ

1. c   2. f   3. b   4. d   5. a   6. e

TRUE/FALSE QUIZ

1. T	5. T	9. T	13. F	17. F
2. F	6. F	10. F	14. T	18. F
3. F	7. T	11. T	15. F	19. T
4. T	8. T	12. F	16. F	20. T

MULTIPLE-CHOICE QUIZ

1. b	4. e	7. e	10. b	13. a
2. a	5. c	8. d	11. c	14. b
3. a	6. d	9. e	12. d	15. c

Chapter 11 Managing Human Resources

SKILL-BUILDING QUIZ

1. B You will keep goodwill and probably find some very good employees, too. A is only a partial answer: You must explain fair hiring practices, especially to employees whose relatives do not measure up, but most will quickly acculturate to this fact of North American work life. C will probably cause ill-will among people who expect their employer to be interested in their concerns.

2. A Tell your mentee exactly what has happened and what you expect him or her to do the next time. This is the most empowering response. Many mentors fail their minority mentees either by failing to give them useful feedback as in B, out of fear that the mentees will find their criticism sexist or racist or, even worse, by overprotecting them as in C.

3. C You should disregard these considerations and base your hiring solely on objective, job-related criteria, without respect to age. This is the only legally correct answer.

4. A "So sorry to ask you to repeat again, but I really want to understand . . ." is the best approach. A translator, as in B. may not help; differently accented English may be the person's native language. C sometimes works, but is risky.

Ferrell, Hirt, Bates & Currie, Business: A Changing World, First Edition

Chapter 12 Customer-Driven Marketing

CHAPTER OUTLINE

Introduction

Nature of Marketing
> The Exchange Relationship
> Marketing Creates Utility
> Functions of Marketing
> The Marketing Concept
> Relationship Marketing

Developing a Marketing Strategy
> Selecting a Target Market
> Developing a Marketing Mix

Marketing Research and Information Systems

Buying Behaviour
> Psychological Variables of Buying Behaviour
> Social Variables of Buying Behaviour
> Understanding Buying Behaviour

The Marketing Environment

CHAPTER OBJECTIVES

After reading this chapter, you should be able to:
- Define marketing and describe the exchange process.
- Specify the functions of marketing.
- Explain the marketing concept and its implications for developing marketing strategies.
- Examine the development of a marketing strategy, including market segmentation and marketing mix.
- Investigate how marketers conduct marketing research and study buying behaviour.
- Summarize the environmental forces that influence marketing decisions.
- Assess a company's marketing plans and propose a solution for resolving its problem.

CHAPTER RECAP

INTRODUCTION

Marketing involves planning and executing the development, pricing, promotion, and distribution of ideas, goods, and services to create exchanges that satisfy individual and organizational goals. Organizations of all sizes and objectives engage in these activities.

Chapter 12 Customer-Driven Marketing

NATURE OF MARKETING

Marketing is a group of activities designed to expedite transactions by creating, distributing, pricing, and promoting goods, services, and ideas. These activities create value by allowing individuals and organizations to obtain what they need and want. Marketing is not manipulation to get consumers to buy products they don't want, nor is it just selling and advertising; it is a systematic approach to satisfying consumers.

At the heart of all business is the **exchange,** the act of giving up one thing (money, credit, labour, goods) in return for something else (goods, services, or ideas). Businesses exchange their goods, services, or ideas for money or credit supplied by customers in a voluntary *exchange relationship.* For an exchange to occur, buyers and sellers must be able to communicate about the "something of value" available to each, and each must be willing to give up its respective "something of value" to receive the "something" held by the other.

What most consumers want is a way to get a job done, solve a problem, or gain some enjoyment. Thus, the tangible product itself may not be as important as the image or the benefits associated with the product.

The central focus of marketing is to create **utility**, which refers to a product's ability to satisfy human needs and wants. **Place utility** is created by making the product available where the buyer wishes to buy it. **Time utility** is created by making a product available when customers wish to purchase it. **Ownership utility** is created by transferring ownership of a product to the buyer. **Form utility** is created through the production process rather than through marketing activities. A key role of marketers is to create place, time, and ownership utility so that human needs and wants are served.

Marketing focuses on a complex set of activities that must be performed to accomplish objectives and generate exchanges. Marketers need to understand buying behaviour so that they can focus on buyers' needs and desires to determine what products to make available. Selling is a persuasive activity accomplished through promotion. Transporting is the process of moving products from the seller to the buyer. Storing is a part of physical distribution and includes warehousing activities. Grading refers to standardizing products and displaying and labeling them so that consumers clearly understand their nature and quality. Financing facilitates the exchange process though providing credit for large purchases. Marketing research allows marketers to determine the need for new products and services. Risk taking is the chance of loss associated with marketing decisions.

A basic philosophy that guides all marketing activities is the **marketing concept,** the idea that an organization should try to satisfy customers' needs through coordinated activities that also allow it to achieve its own goals. The marketing concept suggests that a business should find out what consumers need and want, develop the product that fulfills those needs or wants, and then get the products to the customer. The business must also continually alter, adapt, and develop products to keep pace with changing consumer needs and wants. Although customer satisfaction is the goal of the marketing concept, a company must also achieve its own objectives, such as boosting productivity, reducing costs, or achieving a percentage of a specific market. To implement the marketing concept, a firm must have good information about what consumers want, adopt a consumer orientation, and coordinate its efforts throughout the entire organization; otherwise, it may have too many products that consumers do not want or need.

Chapter 12 Customer-Driven Marketing

Relationship marketing is the process of building intimate customer interactions to maximize customer satisfaction. It continually deepens the customer's dependence on the company and, as the customer's confidence grows, this in turn increases the company's understanding of the customer's needs.

DEVELOPING A MARKETING STRATEGY

To implement the marketing concept, a business needs to develop and maintain a **marketing strategy,** a plan of action for developing, pricing, distributing, and promoting products that meet the needs of specific customers. This definition has two major components: selecting a target market and developing an appropriate marketing mix to satisfy that target market.

A **market** is a group of people who have a need, purchasing power, and the desire and authority to spend money on goods, services, and ideas. A **target market** is a more specific group of consumers on whose needs and wants a company focuses its marketing efforts. Some firms use a **total-market approach** in which they try to appeal to everyone and assume that all buyers have similar needs and wants. Most firms use **market segmentation,** dividing the total market into groups of people who have relatively similar product needs. A **market segment** is a collection of individuals, groups, or organizations that share one or more characteristics and thus have relatively similar product needs and desires. In the **concentration approach,** a company develops one marketing strategy for a single market segment. In the **multisegment approach,** the marketer aims its marketing efforts at two or more segments, developing a marketing strategy for each. For a firm to use the concentration or multisegment approach successfully, several requirements must be met: (1) consumers' needs for the product must be heterogeneous; (2) the segments must be identifiable and divisible; (3) the total market must be divided to allow estimated sales potential, cost, and profits of the segments to be compared; (4) at least one segment must have enough profit potential to justify developing and maintaining a special marketing strategy; and (5) the firm must be able to reach the chosen market segment with a particular marketing strategy. Businesses segment markets on the basis of several variables: demographics (age, sex, race, income, education, occupation, and so on), geography (terrain, climate, etc.), psychographics (personality characteristics, motives, and lifestyles), and behaviouristic characteristics (how the consumer's behaviour toward the product affects its use).

The second step in developing a marketing strategy is to create and maintain a satisfying **marketing mix,** which refers to four marketing activities--product, price, distribution, and promotion--that the firm can control to achieve specific goals within a dynamic marketing environment.

A product--whether a good, a service, an idea, or some combination--is a complex mix of tangible and intangible attributes that provide satisfaction and benefits. Products are among a firm's most visible contacts with consumers. If they do not meet consumer needs and expectations, sales will be difficult, and product life spans will be brief. The product is an important variable of the marketing mix; price, promotion, and distribution issues must be coordinated with product decisions.

Almost anything can be assessed by a **price,** a value placed on an object exchanged between a buyer and a seller. Price quantifies value and is the basis of most market exchanges. It is a key element of the marketing mix because it relates directly to the generation of revenue and profits. Prices can be changed quickly to stimulate demand or respond to competitors' actions.

Chapter 12 Customer-Driven Marketing

Distribution is making products available to customers in the quantities desired. Intermediaries, usually wholesalers and retailers, perform many of the activities required to move products efficiently from producers to consumers or industrial buyers. These involve transporting, warehousing, materials handling, inventory control, and packaging and communication. Eliminating wholesalers and other intermediaries would not lower prices for consumers, as many critics suggest, because the functions these middlemen perform cannot be eliminated.

Promotion is a persuasive form of communication that attempts to expedite a marketing exchange by influencing individuals, groups, and organizations to accept goods, services, and ideas. Promotion includes advertising, personal selling, publicity, and sales promotion.

MARKETING RESEARCH AND INFORMATION SYSTEMS

Marketing research is a systematic, objective process of getting information about potential customers to guide marketing decisions. This research is vital because the marketing concept cannot be implemented without information about customers. A **marketing information system** is a framework for accessing information about customers from sources both inside and outside the organization. This information is important to planning and marketing strategy development. Two types of data are usually available to decision makers. **Primary data** are observed, recorded, or collected directly from respondents; **secondary data** are compiled inside or outside the organization for some purpose other than changing the current situation.

BUYING BEHAVIOUR

Buying behaviour refers to the decision processes and actions of people who purchase and use products. It includes the behaviour of both consumers purchasing products for personal or household use and organizations buying products for business use. Marketers analyze buying behaviour because a firm's marketing strategy should be guided by an understanding of buyers.

Psychological and social variables are important to an understanding of buying behaviour. Psychological factors include **perception**--the process by which a person selects, organizes, and interprets information received from his or her senses; motivation--an inner drive that directs a person's behaviour towards goals; **learning**--changes in a person's behaviour based on information and experience; **attitude**--knowledge and positive or negative feelings about something; and **personality**--the organization of a person's distinguishing character traits, attitudes, and habits. Social factors include **social roles**--the set of expectations for individuals based on some position they occupy; **reference groups**--families, professional groups, civic organizations, and other groups with whom buyers identify and whose values or attitudes they adopt; **social classes**--determined by ranking people into higher or lower positions of respect; and **culture**--the integrated, accepted pattern of human behaviour, including thought, speech, beliefs, actions, and artifacts.

Marketers may not be able to determine accurately what is highly satisfying to buyers, but they know that trying to understand consumer wants and needs is the best way to satisfy them.

Chapter 12 Customer-Driven Marketing

THE MARKETING ENVIRONMENT

The marketing environment influences and structures the development of marketing strategy. Political, legal, and regulatory forces; social forces; competitive and economic forces; and technological forces shape the marketing environment. The forces in the marketing environment are sometimes called uncontrollables, yet they are not totally uncontrollable.

ENHANCEMENT EXERCISES

1. The following is a role-play that allows students to take over as educators. The students are to be broken up into groups and assigned the task of educating Bill on the benefits of a marketing information system and selling him on why their consulting company is the best to hire. Students should be encouraged to make posters and diagrams and/or specialize in an area of marketing research to distinguish their companies from the others. The time limit for the activity should not exceed 30 minutes followed by a five to eight minute presentation.

Situation:

Bill owns a small company that provids people with the knowledge, tools and parts to build their own home computer at significant savings. To date his sales have moved rapidly from $35,000 in year one to $250,000 in year three. Bill is interested in expanding his product line to possible home built DVD kits but is not sure if a market exists.

To date Bill has been running the marketing and product development section of the company solely on intuition. His daughter, Grace, has recently returned home for the summer from Mount Saint Vincent University and has expressed great dismay that Bill lacks any type of MIS system. Bill, who frowns on formal business structure and wasting money, doesn't see much benefit from the establishment of such a system.

To satisfy his daughter he has agreed to listen to a series of presentations from several consulting firms that specialize in the establishment of MIS systems.

As a consulting company you have two chief goals in your brief presentation:

1) Highlight the importance of an MIS System to Bill and his company.
2) Inform Bill of why your company is the best fit for the job.

Please remember:
Bill is a simple and stubborn man. In order for him to understand the benefits, groups should be sure to include examples, diagrams and a strong sales pitch.

The presentation cannot exceed 8 minutes.

Chapter 12 Customer-Driven Marketing

MATCHING QUIZ

Match the following statements with the correct key term.
a. marketing concept
b. marketing strategy
c. market segmentation
d. marketing mix
e. marketing research

_____ 1.   Four marketing activities--product, price, promotion, and distribution--that the firm can control to achieve specific goals within a dynamic marketing environment.

_____ 2.   The idea that an organization should try to satisfy customers' needs through coordinated activities that also allow it to achieve its own goals.

_____ 3.   The practice of dividing the total market into groups of people who have relatively similar product needs.

_____ 4.   A systematic, objective process of getting information about potential customers to guide marketing decisions.

_____ 5.   A plan of action for developing, pricing, distributing, and promoting products that meet the needs of specific customers.

TRUE/FALSE QUIZ

Indicate whether each of the following statements is true or false.

_____ 1.   Ownership utility is created by the production process.

_____ 2.   Learning is a change in a person's behaviour caused by information and experience.

_____ 3.   Grading refers to standardizing products and displaying and labeling them so that consumers clearly understand their nature and quality.

_____ 4.   Trying to determine customers' needs is easy because marketers fully understand what motivates people to buy things.

_____ 5.   Relationship marketing is the process of building intimate customer interactions to maximize customer satisfaction.

_____ 6.   According to the marketing concept, businesses must find out what consumers need and want and develop products that fill those needs and wants.

_____ 7.   Personality may determine the type of car or clothing one buys.

Ferrell, Hirt, Bates & Currie, Business: A Changing World, First Edition

Chapter 12 Customer-Driven Marketing

_____8.   Eliminating wholesalers and retailers would not lower prices for consumers, as some critics believe.

_____9.   Marketing activities are carried out only by business organizations in the pursuit of profit objectives.

_____10.   A market segment is a specific group of consumers on whose needs and wants a company focuses its marketing efforts.

_____11.   Price is always the central focus of the marketing mix.

_____12.   Technology and the economy are part of the marketing environment.

_____13.   Marketing is manipulation to get consumers to buy products they don't need or want.

_____14.   In the total-market approach, a company develops one marketing strategy for a single market segment.

_____15.   The forces in the marketing environment are uncontrollable.

_____16.   Secondary data are observed, recorded, or collected directly from respondents.

_____17.   In order for an exchange to occur, each party must have and be willing to give up something of value.

_____18.   One of the requirements for using the concentration or the multisegment approach to market segmentation is that at least one segment must have enough profit potential to justify developing and maintaining a special marketing strategy.

_____19.   Psychographic bases for segmenting markets relate to some characteristic of the consumer's behavior toward the product.

_____20.   A marketing information system is a framework for managing and structuring primary and secondary data.

Chapter 12 Customer-Driven Marketing

MULTIPLE-CHOICE QUIZ

Choose the correct answer for each of the following questions.

____1. Which of the following is a collection of individuals, groups, or organizations who share one or more characteristics and thus have relatively similar product needs and desires?
   a. market segment
   b. market
   c. target market
   d. total market
   e. multisegment

____2. Which of the following can be changed quickly?
   a. product
   b. distribution
   c. promotion
   d. advertising
   e. price

____3. Which of the following marketing functions may involve providing credit to expedite purchases?
   a. marketing research
   b. financing
   c. grading
   d. buying
   e. selling

____4. Which of the following tries to expedite marketing exchanges by persuading consumers to accept goods, services, or ideas?
   a. product
   b. distribution
   c. price
   d. selling
   e. promotion

Chapter 12 Customer-Driven Marketing

_____5.   Which approach to selecting a target market would most likely be used by General
           Motors in selling its cars and trucks?
           a.   total-market approach
           b.   concentration approach
           c.   multisegment approach
           d.   target-market
           e.   quality approach

_____6.   Which approach to selecting a target market would most likely be used by Imperial
           Sugar in selling its sugar products?
           a.   market segmentation approach
           b.   multisegment approach
           c.   concentration approach
           d.   total-market approach
           e.   quality approach

_____7.   Which of the following is created when the local bank offers automatic teller machines
           in a local convenience store?
           a.   form utility
           b.   place utility
           c.   time utility
           d.   possession utility
           e.   structure utility

_____8.   Which of the following variables affecting buying behaviour is knowledge and
           positive or negative feelings about something?
           a.   personality
           b.   attitude
           c.   learning
           d.   perception
           e.   culture

_____9.   Which of the following is NOT an aspect of distribution?
           a.   transporting
           b.   materials handling
           c.   production
           d.   inventory control
           e.   warehousing

Chapter 12 Customer-Driven Marketing

____10.   Which of the following is created when an automobile dealer transfers the title to a new car to the purchaser of the car?
a.   form utility
b.   place utility
c.   time utility
d.   exchange utility
e.   ownership utility

____11.   Which of the following variables affecting buying behaviour is the integrated, accepted pattern of human behaviour, including thought, speech, beliefs, actions, and artifacts?
a.   culture
b.   social class
c.   reference groups
d.   motivation
e.   social roles

____12.   If Subway introduced a fried chicken product, which of the following marketing environment forces would affect the marketing strategies of KFC (Kentucky Fried Chicken)?
a.   political and legal
b.   economic
c.   social
d.   competitive
e.   technological

____13.   Which of the following is NOT a function of marketing?
a.   buying
b.   storing
c.   manufacturing
d.   marketing research
e.   transporting

____14.   Which of the following is the idea that an organization should try to satisfy customers' needs through coordinated activities that also allow it to achieve its own goals?
a.   marketing concept
b.   marketing research
c.   market segmentation
d.   target marketing
e.   marketing

Chapter 12 Customer-Driven Marketing

_____15.   Which of the following is an example of secondary marketing research data?
        a. observation of shoppers in a grocery stores
        b. mail surveys
        c. telephone surveys
        d. counting the number of coupons redeemed for a product
        e. U.S. Census data

SKILL-BUILDING QUIZ

In the "Build Your Skills" exercise, you practiced analyzing marketing strategies of some well-known companies to determine which of the four marketing mix variables received the most emphasis. Continue that exercise by evaluating the examples below and indicating which variable is receiving the most emphasis.

a. product
b. price
c. distribution
d. promotion`

_____1.   Several airlines, including Air Canada, have set up "pages" on the Internet's World Wide Web. Consumers with Internet access and Web browser software can access these pages to learn about Air Canada, study flight schedules, and reserve flights on Air Canada.

_____2.   The state of Texas created the "Don't Mess with Texas" campaign to fight a highway litter problem. After finding that the primary litterers were blue-collar men age 18-35, the state asked popular Texas musicians, sports heroes, and cartoon characters to voice the message not to "mess with Texas" by littering on roadsides. The antilitter message also appears on road signs, bumper stickers, T-shirts, trash bags, and more. The campaign, which has been successful in terms of both highway litter reduction and popularity among Texans, continues to spread the message a decade after its creation.

_____3.   To get an edge on the competition, one service provider recently modified its rate structure for Internet access. This move undercuts a new online service. Other online services have also made changes in their rate structure to attract new users.

_____4.   Nabisco has introduced a line of snacks, called SnackWells, to appeal to nutrition- and fat-and-calorie-conscious consumers. The cookies and crackers have fewer calories and less fat than regular snacks. They are marketed with humorous advertisements and priced competitively, albeit slightly more expensively than regular snacks.

Chapter 12 Customer-Driven Marketing

ANSWERS

MATCHING QUIZ

1. d   2. a   3. c   4. e   5. b

TRUE/FALSE QUIZ

1. F	5. T	9. F	13. F	17. T
2. T	6. T	10. F	14. F	18. T
3. T	7. T	11. F	15. F	19. F
4. F	8. T	12. T	16. F	20. T

MULTIPLE-CHOICE QUIZ

1. a	4. e	7. b	10. e	13. c
2. e	5. c	8. b	11. a	14. a
3. b	6. d	9. c	12. d	15. e

SKILL-BUILDING QUIZ

1. c   2. d   3. b   4. a

Chapter 13 Dimensions of Marketing Strategy

CHAPTER OUTLINE

Introduction

The Marketing Mix

Product Strategy
      Developing New Products
      Classifying Products
      Product Line and Product Mix
      Product Life Cycle
      Identifying Products

Pricing Strategy
      Pricing Objectives
      Pricing Strategies

Distribution Strategy
      Marketing Channels
      Intensity of Market Coverage
      Physical Distribution
      Importance of Distribution in a Marketing Strategy

Promotion Strategy
      The Promotion Mix
      Promotion Strategies: To Push or Pull
      Objectives of Promotion
      Promotional Positioning

CHAPTER OBJECTIVES

After reading this chapter, you should be able to:
- Describe the role of product in the marketing mix, including how products are developed, classified, and identified.
- Define price and discuss its importance in the marketing mix, including various pricing strategies a firm might employ.
- Identify factors affecting distribution decisions, such as marketing channels and intensity of market coverage.
- Specify the activities involved in promotion, as well as promotional strategies and promotional positioning.
- Evaluate an organization's marketing strategy plans.

Chapter 13 Dimensions of Marketing Strategy

CHAPTER RECAP

THE MARKETING MIX

The key to developing a marketing strategy is maintaining the right marketing mix that satisfies the target market and creates long-term relationships with customers. To develop meaningful customer relationships, marketers have to develop and manage the dimensions of the marketing mix to give their firm an advantage over competitors.

PRODUCT STRATEGY

The term *product* refers to goods, services, and ideas. Because the product is often the most visible of the marketing mix dimensions, managing product decisions is crucial.

To introduce a new product, a business generally follows a multistep process: idea development, idea screening, business analysis, product development, test marketing, and commercialization. New ideas can come from marketing research engineers, and outside sources such as advertising agencies, management consultants, or customers. In the idea-screening phase, marketers look at the organization's resources and objectives; assess their ability to produce and market the product; and consider consumer desires, competition, technological changes, social trends, and political, economic, and environmental considerations. Business analysis is a basic assessment of a product's compatibility in the marketplace and its potential profitability. In the product-development stage, the idea is developed into a prototype, and various elements of the marketing mix are developed for testing. **Test marketing** is a trial minilaunch of a product in limited areas that represent the potential market, allowing a complete test of the marketing strategy in a natural environment. **Commercialization** is the full introduction of a complete marketing strategy and the launch of the product for commercial success.

Products are classified as either consumer products or industrial products. **Consumer products** are for household or family use; they are not intended for any purpose other than daily living. They can be further classified on the basis of consumers' buying behaviour and intentions. Convenience products are bought frequently without a lengthy search and often for immediate consumption. Shopping products are purchased after consumers have compared competitive products and shopped around. Specialty products require even greater research and shopping effort.

Industrial products are used directly or indirectly in the operation or manufacturing processes of businesses. Industrial products are also divided into several categories. Raw materials are natural products taken from the earth and oceans and recycled solid waste. Major equipment is large, expensive items used in production. Accessory equipment includes items used for production, office, or management purposes that usually do not become part of the final product. Component parts are finished items, ready to be assembled into the company's final products. Processed materials are used directly in production or management operations but are not readily identifiable as component parts. Supplies include materials that make production, management, and other operations possible. Industrial services include financial consulting, legal, marketing research, janitorial, and exterminating services.

Chapter 13 Dimensions of Marketing Strategy

A **product line** is a group of closely related products that are treated as a unit because of similar marketing strategy, production, or end-use considerations. A **product mix** is all the products offered by an organization.

There are four stages in the life cycle of a product: introduction, growth, maturity, and decline. The stage a product is in helps determine marketing strategy. In the introductory stage, consumer awareness and acceptance of the new product are limited, sales are zero, and profits are negative because of research and development expenses for the product. Marketers focus on making consumers aware of the product and its benefits during the introductory stage. Sales increase rapidly and profits peak during the growth stage, then start to decline as new companies enter the market, driving prices down and increasing marketing expenses. During the growth stage, the firm tries to strengthen its position in the market by emphasizing the product's benefits and identifying market segments that want these benefits. Sales continue to increase at the beginning of the maturity stage, but then the sales curve peaks and starts to decline while profits continue to decline. This stage is characterized by severe competition and heavy marketing expenditures. During the decline stage, sales continue to fall rapidly, and profits decline and may become losses as prices are cut and necessary marketing expenditures are made.

Branding, packaging, and labeling identify or distinguish one product from others and thus are key marketing activities that help position a product appropriately for its target market.

Branding is the process of naming and identifying products. Identification may occur through a brand (a name, term, symbol, design, or combination that identifies a product and distinguishes it from other products), a brand name (the part of the brand that can be spoken and consists of letters, words, and numbers), a brand mark (the part of the brand that is a distinctive design), and/or a **trademark** (a brand that is registered with the U.S. Patent and Trademark Office and is thus legally protected from use by any other firm). Two major categories of brands are private distributor brands and manufacturer brands. **Manufacturer brands** are initiated and owned by the manufacturer to identify products from the point of production to the point of purchase. **Private distributor brands,** which may be less expensive than manufacturer brands, are owned and controlled by a wholesaler or retailer. **Generic products** have no brand name at all. Marketers may give each product within its complete product mix its own brand name or develop a family of brands with each of the firm's products carrying the same name or at least part of the name.

The **packaging,** or external container that holds and describes the product, influences consumers' attitudes and their buying decisions. A package can perform several functions, including protection, economy, convenience, and promotion.

Labeling, the presentation of important information on the package, is closely associated with packaging. The content of labeling, often required by law, may include ingredients or content, nutrition facts, care instructions, suggestions for use, the manufacturer's address and toll-free number, and other useful information.

Quality reflects the degree to which a good, service, or idea meets the demands and requirements of customers. Quality has become a key means for differentiating products in consumers' minds.

Chapter 13 Dimensions of Marketing Strategy

PRICING STRATEGY

Price, the value placed on an object exchanged between a buyer and a seller, is probably the most flexible variable in the marketing mix.

Pricing objectives specify the role of price in an organization's marketing mix and strategy. These objectives are usually influenced not only by marketing mix decisions but also by finance, accounting, and production factors. Maximizing profits and sales, boosting market share, maintaining the status quo, and survival are common pricing objectives.

Pricing strategies provide guidelines for achieving the company's pricing objectives and overall marketing strategy; they specify how price will be used as a variable in the marketing mix. Setting the price for a new product is critical: The right price leads to profitability; the wrong price may kill the product. There are two basic strategies to setting the price for a new product. **Price skimming** is charging the highest possible price that buyers who want the product will pay, while a **penetration price** is a low price designed to help a product enter the market and gain market share rapidly. Penetration pricing is less flexible than price skimming; it is more difficult to raise a penetration price than to lower a skimming price. **Psychological pricing** encourages purchases based on emotional rather than rational responses to the price. Even/odd pricing assumes that consumers will buy more of a product priced at $9.99 than at $10 because the product seems a bargain at the lower odd price. Symbolic/prestige pricing assumes that high prices connote high quality. Temporary price reductions, or **discounts,** are often employed to boost sales. Although there are many types of price discounts, quantity, seasonal, and promotional discounts are widely used.

DISTRIBUTION STRATEGY

The best products in the world will not be successful unless companies make them available where and when customers want to buy them.

A **marketing channel,** or channel of distribution, is a group of organizations that move products from their producer to customers. Such organizations are called *middlemen,* or intermediaries. Two intermediary organizations are retailers and wholesalers. **Retailers** buy products from manufacturers (or other intermediaries) and sell them to consumers for home and household use rather than for resale or for use in producing other products. Retailing usually occurs in a store, but may also take place through the Internet, vending machines, mail-order catalogs, and entertainment. By bringing together an assortment of products from competing producers, retailers create place, time, and ownership utility. Competition between different types of stores is changing the nature of retailing. **Wholesalers** are intermediaries who buy from producers or from other wholesalers and sell to retailers. Although it is true that wholesalers can be eliminated, their functions must be passed on to some other entity, such as the producer, another intermediary, or even the customer. **Supply chain management** refers to long-term partnerships among marketing channel members working together to reduce costs, waste, and unnecessary movement in the channel in order to satisfy customers.

Typical marketing channels for consumer products were shown in Figure 13.3 of your text. In Channel A, the product moves from the producer directly to the consumer. In Channel B, the product goes from producer to retailer to consumer. In Channel C, the product is handled by a wholesaler and a retailer before it reaches the consumer. In Channel D, the product goes to an agent, a wholesaler, and a retailer

Chapter 13 Dimensions of Marketing Strategy

before going to the consumer. Services are usually distributed through direct marketing channels because they are generally produced *and* consumed simultaneously.

A major distribution decision is how many and what type of outlets should carry the product. The intensity of market coverage depends on buyer behaviour and the nature of the target market and the competition. **Intensive distribution** makes a product available in as many outlets as possible. Because availability is important to purchasers of convenience products, a nearby location with a minimum of time spent searching and waiting in line is most important to the consumer. **Selective distribution** uses only a small number of all available outlets to expose products. It is used most often for products for which consumers buy only after shopping and comparing price, quality, and style. **Exclusive distribution** exists when a manufacturer gives a middleman the sole right to sell a product in a defined geographic territory. Exclusive distribution is the opposite of intensive distribution in that products are purchased and consumed over a long period of time, and service or information are required to develop a satisfactory sales relationship.

Physical distribution is all the activities necessary to move products from producers to customers-- inventory control, transportation, warehousing, and materials handling. It creates time and place utility by making products available when they are wanted, with adequate service and at minimum cost. Both goods and services require physical distribution. **Transportation,** the shipment of products to buyers, creates time and place utility for products, and thus is a key element in the flow of goods and services from producer to consumer. Five major modes of transportation used to move products are railways, motor vehicles, inland waterways, pipelines, and airways. Factors affecting the selection of a mode of transportation include cost, capability to handle the product, reliability, and availability. **Warehousing** is the design and operation of facilities to receive, store, and ship products. Regardless of whether a private or a public warehouse is used, warehousing is important because it makes products available for shipment to match demand at different geographic locations. **Materials handling** is the physical handling and movement of products in warehousing and transportation. Well-coordinated loading and movement systems increase efficiency and reduce costs.

Distribution decisions are among the least flexible marketing mix decisions. They often commit resources and establish contractual relationships that are difficult if not impossible to change.

PROMOTION STRATEGY

The role of promotion is to communicate with individuals, groups, and organizations to facilitate an exchange directly or indirectly. Promotion is used not only to sell products but also to influence opinions and attitudes toward an organization, person, or cause. The role that these elements play in a marketing strategy is extremely important.

Advertising, personal selling, publicity, and sales promotion are collectively known as the promotion mix because a strong promotion program results from the careful selection and blending of these elements. Coordinating the promotion mix elements and synchronizing promotion as a unified effort is called **integrated marketing communications**.

Advertising is a paid form of nonpersonal communication transmitted through a mass medium, such as television commercials, magazine advertisements, or online ads. Advertising media are the vehicles or forms of communication used to reach a desired audience--newspapers, magazines, direct mail,

Chapter 13 Dimensions of Marketing Strategy

billboards, television, radio, and cyber ads. Infomercials are large blocks of radio or television air time featuring a celebrity or upbeat host talking about and demonstrating a product.

Personal selling is direct, two-way communication with buyers and potential buyers. For many products--especially large, expensive ones with specialized uses, such as cars and houses--interaction between a salesperson and the customer is probably the most important promotional tool. Personal selling is the most flexible of the promotional methods because it gives marketers the greatest opportunity to communicate specific information that might trigger a purchase; it is also one of the most costly forms of promotion. There are three distinct categories of salespersons: order takers, creative salespersons, and support salespersons. For most of these salespeople, personal selling is a six-step process: prospecting (identifying potential buyers), approaching (using a referral or calling on a customer without prior notice to determine interest in the product), presenting (getting the prospect's attention with a product demonstration), handling objections (countering reasons for not buying the product), closing (asking the prospect to buy the product), and following up (checking customer satisfaction with the purchased product).

Publicity is nonpersonal communication transmitted through the mass media but not paid for directly by the firm. A firm does not pay the media cost for publicity and is not identified as the originator of the message; instead, the message is presented in news story form. Many companies have *public relations* departments to try to gain favorable publicity and minimize negative publicity for the firm. Although publicity and advertising are both carried by the mass media, they differ in several major ways. Advertising, personal selling, and sales promotion are especially useful for influencing exchanges directly. Publicity is extremely important when communication focuses on a company's activities and products and is directed at interest groups, current and potential investors, regulatory agencies, and society in general.

Sales promotion involves direct inducements offering added value or some other incentive for buyers to enter into an exchange. The major tools of sales promotion are store displays, premiums, trading stamps, samples and demonstrations, coupons, contests and sweepstakes, refunds, and trade shows. It is used to enhance and supplement other forms of promotion.

In developing a promotion mix, organizations must decide whether to push or pull the product. A **push strategy** attempts to motivate middlemen to push the product down to their customers. A **pull strategy** uses promotion to create consumer demand for a product so that consumers exert pressure on marketing channel members to make it available. A company can use either strategy, or it can use a variation or combination of the two. The allocation of promotional resources to various marketing mix elements probably determines which strategy a marketer uses.

Firms use promotion for many reasons, but typical objectives are to stimulate demand; to stabilize sales; and to inform, remind, and reinforce customers. Increasing demand for a product is probably the most typical promotional objective. Reinforcement promotion attempts to assure current users of the product that they have made the right choice and tells them how to get the most satisfaction from the product.

Promotional positioning uses promotion to create and maintain an image of a product in buyers' minds. It is a natural result of market segmentation. A promotional strategy helps differentiate the product and make it appeal to a particular market segment.

Chapter 13 Dimensions of Marketing Strategy

ENHANCEMENT EXERCISES

1. Hold an invention contest in class. Form small groups of two and have students invent one to two products and present the idea to classmates. For best results, limit the presentation to one minute then have students vote on the best and worst invention.

MATCHING QUIZ

Match the following statements with the correct key term.

a.   branding
b.   trademark
c.   private distributor brands
d.   manufacturer brands
e.   generic products

_____1.   This brand is initiated and owned by the manufacturer to identify products from the point of production to the point of purchase.

_____2.   A brand that is registered with the Trademarks Office and is thus legally protected from use by any other firm.

_____3.   These have no brand name at all.

_____4.   The process of naming and identifying products.

_____5.   This brand is owned and controlled by a wholesaler or retailer.

TRUE/FALSE QUIZ

Indicate whether each of the following statements is true or false.

_____1.   Convenience products require a special search and effort to obtain.

_____2.   A product mix is a group of closely related products that are treated as a unit because of similar marketing strategy, production, or end-use considerations.

_____3.   Test marketing is a trial minilaunch of a product in limited areas that represent the potential market.

_____4.   Psychological pricing encourages rational responses to product price.

_____5.   Sales promotions are used to enhance and supplement other forms of promotion.

_____6.   Major equipment includes items used for production, office, or management purposes.

Chapter 13 Dimensions of Marketing Strategy

_____7.   Manufacturers are involved in decisions about distribution, promotion, pricing, and product development for manufacturer brands.

_____8.   Publicity is a paid form of nonpersonal communication transmitted through a mass medium.

_____9.   Distribution is the most flexible of the marketing mix variables.

_____10.   Profits for a new product are negative in the introductory stage because of expenses associated with research, development, and marketing.

_____11.   Personal selling is the most flexible of the promotional mix variables.

_____12.   The functions and services provided by intermediaries may be eliminated, thereby saving consumers much money.

_____13.   Shipping is often the least expensive means of transportation.

_____14.   Penetration pricing is charging the highest possible price that buyers who want the product will pay.

_____15.   Packaging serves only a promotional function.

_____16.   Shopping products are typically distributed through selective distribution.

_____17.   Promotional positioning is a natural result of market segmentation.

_____18.   Wholesalers are middlemen who sell products for home and household use rather than for resale.

_____19.   Labeling of content, origin, and instructions for use is often required by the federal government.

_____20.   Penetration pricing is less flexible than price skimming.

MULTIPLE-CHOICE QUIZ

Choose the correct answer for each of the following questions.

_____1.   In what stage of the product life cycle do profits peak?
    a.   introductory stage
    b.   death stage
    c.   maturity stage
    d.   decline stage
    e.   growth stage

Chapter 13 Dimensions of Marketing Strategy

_____2. Which of the following would most likely be used to distribute yachts and airplanes?
   a. market coverage
   b. exclusive distribution
   c. selective distribution
   d. intensive distribution
   e. marketing intermediary

_____3. Which of the following does NOT facilitate an exchange directly?
   a. advertising
   b. personal selling
   c. publicity
   d. sales promotion
   e. none of the above

_____4. In what stage of the new product development process is a prototype developed?
   a. idea development
   b. idea screening
   c. business analysis
   d. product development
   e. test marketing

_____5. Which of the following involves the design and operation of facilities to receive, store, and ship products?
   a. promotion
   b. physical distribution
   c. materials handling
   d. transportation
   e. warehousing

_____6. Which of the following is NOT created by retailers?
   a. time utility
   b. place utility
   c. form utility
   d. ownership utility
   e. All of the above are created by retailers.

_____7. Which of the following is generally a shopping product?
   a. newspaper
   b. stereo
   c. hot-air balloon
   d. milk
   e. soft drink

_____8. Home Depot and other very large specialty stores concentrating on a single product line and competing on the basis of low prices and product availability are examples of
   a. category killers.
   b. catalog showrooms.
   c. warehouse clubs.

Chapter 13 Dimensions of Marketing Strategy

d. superstores.

e. discount stores.

_____9. Which of the following is used most often to distribute products such as candy, produce, and cigarettes?

a. Channel A

b. Channel B

c. Channel C

d. Channel D

e. Channel E

_____10. Which of the following would generally be classified as major equipment?

a. bulldozer

b. software

c. speakers

d. paper clips

e. computer paper

_____11. Which of the following modes of transportation is used most often to transport oil and chemicals?

a. air transport

b. railroads

c. trucks

d. shipping

e. pipelines

_____12. Even/odd pricing is an example of

a. price skimming

b. psychological pricing.

c. penetration pricing.

d. symbolic pricing.

e. pricing objective.

_____13. Which of the following personal-selling steps asks a prospect to buy a product?

a. prospecting

b. presenting

c. closing

d. following up

e. approaching

_____14. Which of the following allows a company to generate much-needed revenue to help offset the costs of research and development of a new product?

a. price skimmmg

b. penetration pricing

c. psychological pricing

d. price discounting

e. even/odd pricing

Chapter 13 Dimensions of Marketing Strategy

_____15.   Which of the following is direct, two-way communication with buyers or potential buyers?
   a. sales promotion
   b. publicity
   c. personal selling
   d. advertising
   e. promotion

SKILL-BUILDING QUIZ

In the "Build Your Skills" exercise, you analyzed the marketing strategy of Canadian Tire. Continue that analysis by answering the following.

_____1.   Which of the following marketing mix elements is the primary focus of Canadian Tire's strategy (e.g., how is Canadian Tire competing against other hotel chains)?
   a. product
   b. price
   c. distribution
   d. promotion

_____2.   Which of the following promotion mix elements does Canadian Tire seem to be relying on in its current marketing strategy?
   a. sales promotion
   b. publicity
   c. personal selling
   d. advertising

_____3.   Briefly describe how Canadian Tire uses each of the marketing strategy elements to appeal to its target market.

   Product: _____

   Price: _____

   Distribution: _____

   Promotion: _____

Chapter 13 Dimensions of Marketing Strategy

ANSWERS

MATCHING QUIZ

1. d   2. b   3. e   4. a   5. c

TRUE/FALSE QUIZ

1. F	5. T	9. F	13. F	17. T
2. F	6. F	10. T	14. F	18. F
3. T	7. T	11. T	15. F	19. T
4. F	8. F	12. F	16. T	20. T

MULTIPLE-CHOICE QUIZ

1. e	4. d	7. b	10. a	13. c
2. b	5. e	8. a	11. e	14. a
3. c	6. c	9. d	12. b	15. c

SKILL-BUILDING QUIZ

1. b   2. d

3. Product: Canadian Tire is famous for having everything and anything you most likely could need, including a gas bar. Forty percent of Canadians shop at Canadian Tire every week.

Price: Canadian Tire offers competitive pricing, and distributes "Canadian Tire" money, which encourages the use of the money for purchasing store merchandise.

Distribution: Canadian Tire locates its' facilities within 15 minutes drive of 85% of Canadians' homes. Nine out of ten Canadians shop at Canadian Tire at least twice a year.

Promotion: Canadian Tire sends the message of family, work, dreams and rewards, supported by their "A Bike Story" national campaign.

Chapter 14 Accounting and Financial Statements

CHAPTER OUTLINE

Introduction

The Nature of Accounting
        Accountants
        Accounting or Bookkeeping?
        The Uses of Accounting Information

The Accounting Process
        The Accounting Equation
        Double-Entry Bookkeeping
        The Accounting Cycle

Financial Statements
        The Income Statement
        The Balance Sheet

Ratio Analysis: Analyzing Financial Statements
        Profitability Ratios
        Asset Utilization Ratios
        Liquidity Ratios
        Debt Utilization Ratios
        Per Share Data
        Industry Analysis

CHAPTER OBJECTIVES

After reading this chapter, you should be able to:
- Define accounting and describe the different uses of accounting information.
- Demonstrate the accounting process.
- Decipher the various components of an income statement in order to evaluate a firm's "bottom line."
- Interpret a company's balance sheet to determine its current financial position.
- Analyze financial statements, using ratio analysis, to evaluate a company's performance.
- Assess a company's financial position using its accounting statements and ratio analysis.

CHAPTER RECAP

INTRODUCTION

Accounting is the financial "language" organizations use to record, measure, and interpret all of their financial transactions and records. All organizations use accounting to ensure they use their money wisely and to plan for the future.

Chapter 14 Accounting and Financial Statements

THE NATURE OF ACCOUNTING

Accounting is the recording, measurement, and interpretation of financial information. People and institutions, both within and outside businesses, use accounting tools to evaluate organizational operations.

Individuals and businesses can hire a **public accountant,** an independent professional, to provide accounting services ranging from the preparation and filing of individual tax returns to complex audits of corporate financial records. A **chartered public accountant (CPA)** has been officially certified in the province in which he or she practices after meeting certain educational and professional requirements established by the province. Certification gives a public accountant the right to officially express an unbiased opinion regarding the accuracy of the client's financial statements. Large corporations, government agencies, and other organizations may employ their own **private accountants** to prepare and analyze their financial statements. Private accountants can be CPAs and may become **certified management accountants (CMAs)** by passing a rigorous examination.

Although the terms *accounting* and *bookkeeping* are often used interchangeably, they do not mean the same thing. Narrower and more mechanical than accounting, bookkeeping is typically limited to the routine, day-to-day recording of business transactions. Accountants not only record financial information, but also understand, interpret, and even develop sophisticated accounting systems necessary to classify and analyze complex financial information.

Accountants summarize the information they derive from a firm's business transactions in various financial statements. Many business failures may be linked directly to ignorance of the trends and other information "hidden" inside these financial statements. Managers and owners use financial statements (1) to aid in internal planning and control and (2) for external purposes such as reporting to the Canadian Customs and Revenue Agency, stockholders, creditors, customers, employees, and other interested parties.

Managerial accounting refers to the internal use of accounting statements by managers in planning and directing the organization's activities. Management's greatest concern is **cash flow,** the movement of money through an organization over a daily, weekly, monthly, or yearly basis. A common reason for a cash shortfall is poor managerial planning. Managerial accounting is the backbone of an organization's **budget,** an internal financial plan that forecasts expenses and income over a set period of time. While most companies prepare master budgets for the entire firm, many also prepare budgets for smaller segments of the organization such as divisions, departments, product lines, or projects. The major value of a budget lies in its breakdown of cash inflows and outflows.

Managers also use accounting statements to report the firm's financial performance to outsiders. They may become the basis for the information provided in the official corporate annual report, a summary of the firm's financial information, products, and growth plans for owners and potential investors. The most important component of an annual report is the CPA's signature attesting that the required financial statements accurately reflect the financial condition of the firm; financial statements meeting these conditions are termed *audited.* The primary external users of audited accounting information are government agencies, shareholders and potential investors, and lenders, suppliers, and employees. Government entities require organizations to file audited financial statements concerning taxes owed and paid, payroll deductions for employees and, for corporations, new issues of securities (stocks and bonds). A corporation's shareholders use financial statements to evaluate the return on their investment

Chapter 14 Accounting and Financial Statements

and the overall quality of the firm's management team; potential investors use them to determine whether the company meets their investment requirements and whether the returns from a given firm are likely to compare favorably with other similar companies. Banks and other lenders look at financial statements to determine a company's ability to meet current and future debt obligations if a loan or credit is granted. Labour unions and employees use financial statements to establish reasonable expectations for salary and other benefit requests.

THE ACCOUNTING PROCESS

Accountants carry out the accounting function by using the accounting equation and double-entry bookkeeping.

Accountants are concerned with an organization's assets, liabilities, and equity. A firm's economic resources, or items of value that it owns, represent its **assets** such as cash, inventory, land, equipment, buildings, and other tangible and intangible things. **Liabilities** are debts the firm owes to others. **Owners' equity** equals assets minus liabilities and reflects historical values. The relationship between assets, liabilities, and owners' equity is a fundamental concept in accounting and is known as the **accounting equation:** assets = liabilities + owners equity.

Double-entry bookkeeping is a system of recording and classifying business transactions in accounts that maintains the balance of the accounting equation. To keep the accounting equation in balance, each business transaction must be recorded in two separate accounts. All business transactions are classified as either assets, liabilities, or owners' equity; but most organizations break down these three accounts further to provide more specific information about a transaction.

In any accounting system, financial data pass through a four-step procedure called the **accounting cycle** because it collects, records, and analyzes raw data constantly throughout the business's life. Financial managers begin the accounting cycle by gathering and examining source documents concerning specific transactions. Each financial transaction is then recorded in a **journal,** a time-ordered list of account transactions. Next, the information is transferred, or posted, to a **general ledger,** a book or computer file with separate sections for each account. At the end of the accounting period, the manager or accountant prepares a trial balance of all the accounts in the general ledger. If the accounting equation is in balance, the information is used to prepare the firms' financial statements. In the case of public corporations and certain other organizations, a CPA must verify that the organization followed acceptable accounting practices in preparing the financial statements. When these statements have been completed, the organization's books are "closed," and the accounting cycle begins anew for the next accounting period.

FINANCIAL STATEMENTS

The end results of the accounting process are a series of financial statements, such as the income statement and the balance sheet. These statements are provided to stockholders and potential investors in a firm's annual report as well as to other relevant outsiders such as creditors and the Canadian Customs and Revenue Agency. Because different organizations generate income in different ways, they may use different formats and terminology in preparing accounting statements. Each type of business uses its own accounting principles, called generally accepted accounting principles (GAAP).

Chapter 14 Accounting and Financial Statements

The **income statement** (also called a profit and loss statement or operating statement) is a financial report that shows an organization's profitability over a period of time. The income statement indicates the firm's profitability or income (the bottom line), which is derived by subtracting the firm's expenses from its revenues.

Revenue is the total amount of money received from the sale of goods or services as well as other business activities, such as the rental of property and investments. Nonbusiness entities typically obtain revenues through donations from individuals and/or grants from governments and private foundations. The next major item included in most income statements is the **cost of goods sold,** the amount of money the firm spent to buy and/or produce the products it sold during the accounting period. **Gross income** is revenues minus the costs of good sold required to generate the revenues.

Expenses are the costs incurred in the day-to-day operations of the organization. The number and type of expense accounts shown on income statements vary from organization to organization, but three common ones are selling, general, and administrative expenses; research, development, and engineering expenses; and interest expense. Included in the general and administrative category is a special type of expense known as **depreciation,** the process of spreading the costs of long-lived assets such as buildings and equipment over the total number of accounting periods in which they are expected to be used.

Net income (or net earnings) is the total profit (or loss) after all expenses, including taxes, have been deducted from revenue. Accountants often divide profits into individual sections such as operating income and earnings before interest and taxes. Income statements may also include previous years' income statements to permit comparison of performance from one period to another.

The second basic financial statement is the **balance sheet,** which presents a "snapshot" of an organization's financial position at a given moment. It indicates what the organization owns or controls and the various sources of the funds used to pay for these assets, such as bank debt or owners' equity. The balance sheet takes its name from its reliance on the accounting equation: Assets *must* equal liabilities plus owners' equity. The balance sheet is an accumulation of all financial transactions conducted by an organization since its founding. Balance sheets can be presented in a vertical format with assets at the top followed by liabilities and owners' equity, or with assets on the left side and liabilities and owners' equity on the right side.

All asset accounts are listed in descending order of *liquidity*--that is, how quickly each could be turned into cash. Short-term, or current, assets are used or converted into cash within the course of a calendar year. Thus, cash is listed first followed by temporary investments, **accounts receivable** (money owed the company by its clients or customers), and inventory (in the form of raw materials, goods in process, and finished products ready for sale). Finally, long-term, or fixed, assets, which represent a commitment of organizational funds of at least one year, are listed.

Assets must be financed, either through borrowing (liabilities) or through owner investments (owners' equity). Current liabilities include a firm's financial obligations to short-term creditors that must be repaid within one year, while long-term liabilities have longer repayment terms. **Accounts payable** represents amounts owed to suppliers for goods and services purchased with credit. Other liabilities include wages owed to employees and taxes owed to the government. Occasionally, these accounts are consolidated into an **accrued expenses** account, representing all unpaid financial obligations incurred by the organization.

Chapter 14 Accounting and Financial Statements

Owners' equity includes the owners' contributions to the organization along with income earned by the organization and retained to finance continued growth and development. The accounts listed in the owners' equity section of the balance sheet may vary from business to business. All equity accounts may be listed in one category or may be divided into the various classes of stock (common and preferred) outstanding.

RATIO ANALYSIS: ANALYZING FINANCIAL STATEMENTS

The income statement and balance sheet together provide the means to answer two critical questions: (1) How much did the firm make or lose? and (2) How much is the firm presently worth based on historical values found on the balance sheet? **Ratio analysis,** calculations that measure an organization's financial health, brings the information from the income statement and balance sheet into sharper focus so that managers, lenders, owners, and other interested parties can measure and compare the organization's productivity, profitability, and financing mix with other similar entities. It is the relationship of the calculated ratios to both prior organizational performance and the performance of the organization's "peers," as well as its stated goals, that matters.

Profitability ratios measure how much operating income or net income an organization is able to generate relative to its assets, owners' equity, and sales. The **profit margin,** computed by dividing net income by sales, shows the overall percentage profits earned by the company. The higher the profit margin, the better the cost controls within the company and the higher the return on every dollar of revenue. **Return on assets,** net income divided by assets, shows how much income the firm produces for every dollar invested in assets. A low return on assets means the company is probably not using its assets very productively. **Return on equity** (also called return on investment (ROI)), calculated by dividing net income by owners' equity, shows how much income is generated by each $1 the owners have invested in the firm. A low return on equity means low shareholder returns.

Asset utilization ratios measure how well a firm uses its assets to generate each $1 of sales. Companies that use their assets more productively will have higher returns on assets than less efficient competitors. The **receivables turnover,** sales divided by accounts receivable, indicates how many times a firm collects its accounts receivable in one year, or how quickly it is able to collect payments on its credit sales. **Inventory turnover,** sales divided by total inventory, indicates how many times a firm sells and replaces its inventory over the course of a year. A high inventory turnover ratio may indicate great efficiency, but may also suggest the possibility of lost sales due to insufficient stock levels. **Total asset turnover,** sales divided by total assets, measures how well an organization uses all of its assets in creating sales. It indicates whether a company is using its assets productively.

Liquidity ratios compare current (short-term) assets to current liabilities to indicate the speed with which a company can turn its assets into cash to pay off debts. High liquidity ratios may satisfy a creditor's need for safety, but ratios that are too high may indicate that current assets are not being used efficiently. Liquidity ratios are best examined in conjunction with asset utilization ratios because high turnover ratios imply that cash is flowing through an organization very quickly--a situation that dramatically reduces the need for the type of reserves measured by liquidity ratios. The **current ratio** is calculated by dividing current assets by current liabilities. The **quick ratio** (or **acid test**) is a more stringent measure of liquidity because it eliminates inventory, the least liquid current asset.

Debt utilization ratios provide information about how much debt an organization is using relative to other sources of capital, such as owners' equity. Because the use of debt carries an interest charge that must be paid regularly regardless of profitability, debt financing is much riskier than equity. Consequently, the managers of most firms tend to keep debt-to-asset levels below 50 percent. The **debt to total assets ratio** indicates how much of the firm is financed by debt and how much by owners' equity. The **times interest earned ratio,** operating income divided by interest expenses, is a measure of the safety margin a company has with respect to the interest payments it must make to its creditors. A low times interest earned ratio indicates that even a small decrease in earnings may lead to financial difficulties.

Investors may use **per share data** to compare the performance of one company with another on an equal, or per share, basis. **Earnings per share,** net income or profit divided by the number of shares of stock outstanding, is important because it is yearly changes in earnings per share, in combination with other economic factors, that determine a company's overall stock price. **Dividends per share,** the actual before-tax cash payment received for each share owned, is another way to analyze the overall return resulting from a stockholder's investment.

While comparing a firm's performance to previous years is an excellent gauge of whether corporate operations are improving or deteriorating, another way to analyze a firm is to compare its performance with other firms in its industry.

ENHANCEMENT EXERCISE

Almost every large company publishes an annual report on the Internet with their balance sheet and income statement in the financial section. Examine a few companies that operate in similar industries such as Dell and Hewlett Packer or Sears and Wal-Mart and calculate several ratios. Determine which company appears to be the best suited for continued prosperity and highlight any apparent problems. Have classmates conduct the same analysis and compare the results.

MATCHING QUIZ

Match the following statements with the correct key term.

a. profitability ratios
b. asset utilization ratios
c. liquidity ratios
d. debt utilization ratios
e. per share data

____1.   These ratios compare current assets to current liabilities to indicate the speed with which a company can turn its assets into cash to meet short-term debt.

____2.   These ratios measure how well a firm uses its assets to generate each $1 of sales.

____3.   These ratios provide information about how much debt an organization is using relative to other sources of capital.

____4.   These ratios measure how much operating income or net income an organization is

Chapter 14 Accounting and Financial Statements

able to generate relative to its assets, owners' equity, and sales.

_____5.   These ratios are used to compare the performance of one company with another on an equal basis.

TRUE/FALSE QUIZ

Indicate whether each of the following statements is true or false.

_____1.   A highly successful and rapidly growing business can be struggling to make payments to suppliers and lenders because of inadequate cash flow.

_____2.   The balance sheet represents the result of transactions for a specific month, quarter, or year.

_____3.   If a business generates income of $5,000 by selling $3,500 worth of inventory during an accounting period, the bookkeeper or financial manager must debit one account and credit another.

_____4.   The return on equity ratio shows how much income the firm produces for every dollar invested in assets.

_____5.   After examining source documents to determine their effect on the asset, liability, and owners' equity accounts, managers next record each transaction in the general ledger.

_____6.   All organizations, regardless of size, have need of the financial information compiled by accountants.

_____7.   In the accounting equation, assets equal liabilities plus owners' equity.

_____8.   The acid test shows how fast a company can turn its most current assets into cash to pay off its short-term debts.

_____9.   Private accountants are independent professionals who provide accounting services for a fee.

_____10.   Depreciation is the process of spreading the costs of long-lived assets such as buildings and equipment over the total number of accounting periods in which they are expected to be used.

_____11.   Accounts receivable represents amounts owed to the company and includes an allowance for bad debts.

_____12.   The more assets a business finances with debt, the less risk the business may be exposed to.

_____13.   The income statement shows whether the firm made a profit.

Chapter 14 Accounting and Financial Statements

____14.	The income statement is a snapshot of a company's financial position at a given moment.

____15.	The higher a company's profit margin, the better is its cost control and the higher is the return on every dollar of revenue.

____16.	Most businesses try to keep their debt to asset ratios above 50 percent.

____17.	Businesses want less cash coming into the business than needed to cover incoming bills.

____18.	Net income is the profit left after all expenses have been deducted from revenue.

____19.	Liquidity ratios measure how much operating income or net income a firm can generate relative to its assets, owners' equity, and sales.

____20.	Dividends per share is the actual before-tax cash payment received for each share of stock owned.

MULTIPLE-CHOICE QUIZ

Choose the correct answer for each of the following questions.

____1.	A book or computer file with separate sections for each account is called a
	a.	balance sheet.
	b.	receipt.
	c.	trial balance.
	d.	journal.
	e.	general ledger.

____2.	Which of the following compares current assets to current liabilities to indicate the speed with which a company can turn its assets into cash to pay off its debts?
	a.	liquidity ratios
	b.	profitability ratios
	c.	asset utilization ratios
	d.	debt utilization ratios
	e.	per share data

____3.	Which of the following is calculated by dividing net income by the number of shares outstanding?
	a.	profit margin per share
	b.	dividends per share
	c.	earnings per share
	d.	book value per share
	e.	return on equity per share

Chapter 14 Accounting and Financial Statements

_____4.   Which of the following is an independent professional who provides accounting services to businesses and individuals for a fee?
   a.   public accountant
   b.   certified public accountant
   c.   private accountant
   d.   certified management accountant
   e.   none of the above

_____5.   Which of the following is the most liquid of the current assets on a balance sheet?
   a.   temporary investments
   b.   inventory
   c.   accounts receivable
   d.   bad debts
   e.   cash

_____6.   Which of the following can tell analysts how much debt a company is using relative to other sources of capital?
   a.   per share data
   b.   debt utilization ratios
   c.   asset utilization ratios
   d.   liquidity ratios
   e.   profitability ratios

_____7.   Which of the following forecasts expenses and income over a set period of time?
   a.   master budget
   b.   budget
   c.   income statement
   d.   balance sheet
   e.   cash flow

_____8.   Which of the following represents amounts owed to a company's suppliers?
   a.   depreciation expense
   b.   liabilities
   c.   accrued expense
   d.   accounts payable
   e.   accounts receivable

_____9.   Which of the following is NOT included on a balance sheet?
   a.   accounts receivable
   b.   accounts payable
   c.   stockholders' equity
   d.   cost of goods sold
   e.   notes payable

Chapter 14 Accounting and Financial Statements

_____10.   Which of the following is NOT an external user of financial statements?
    a. Canadian Customs and Revenue Agency
    b. financial institutions
    c. managers
    d. shareholders
    e. creditors

_____11.   Which of the following measures how much operating or net income a firm can generate relative to its assets, owners' equity, and sales?
    a. asset utilization ratios
    b. debt utilization ratios
    c. profitability ratios
    d. per share data
    e. liquidity ratios

_____12.   Which of the following shows how much income a firm produces for every dollar invested in assets?
    a. return on assets
    b. return on equity
    c. return on the dollar
    d. return on inventory
    e. total asset turnover

_____13.   Which of the following is NOT included on an income statement?
    a. net income
    b. expenses
    c. depreciation expense
    d. accounts receivable
    e. revenue

_____14.   Which of the following measures how efficiently a firm uses its assets to generate each $1 of sales?
    a. debt utilization ratios
    b. asset utilization ratios
    c. liquidity ratios
    d. inventory turnover
    e. profitability ratios

_____15.   Which of the following is calculated by dividing net income by sales?
    a. quick ratio
    b. total asset turnover ratio
    c. return on equity ratio
    d. return on assets ratio
    e. profit margin

Chapter 14 Accounting and Financial Statements

SKILL-BUILDING QUIZ

In the "Build Your Skills" exercise of your text, you practiced financial analysis using the figures for the hypothetical NewNet Productions Ltd. Continue building on these skills by choosing the best answer for each of the following (use the numbers provided in the text to make calculations).

____1.   What is NewNet Productions' total asset turnover?
      a.   14.9
      b.   1.49
      c.   149.0
      d.   .149

____2.   What is NewNet Productions' times interest earned ratio?
      a.   3.21
      b.   .321
      c.   32.1
      d.   13.2

____3.   Evaluate NewNet Productions' current ratio.
      a.   Cannot be calculated with the information provided.
      b.   The firm has an acceptable ratio.
      c.   The firm has a high ratio.
      d.   The firm has a low ratio.

____4.   Assume NewNet Productions has receivables of $1,500,000. Calculate its receivables turnover.
      a.   .42
      b.   Cannot be calculated.
      c.   2.4
      d.   4.2

ANSWERS

MATCHING QUIZ

1. c   2. b   3. d   4. a   5. e

TRUE/FALSE QUIZ

1. T	5. F	9. F	13. T	17. F
2. F	6. T	10. T	14. F	18. T
3. T	7. T	11. T	15. T	19. F
4. F	8. T	12. F	16. F	20. T

Chapter 14 Accounting and Financial Statements

MULTIPLE-CHOICE QUIZ

1. e	4. a	7. b	10. c	13. d
2. a	5. e	8. d	11. c	14. b
3. c	6. b	9. d	12. a	15. e

SKILL-BUILDING QUIZ

1. b   2. c   3. a   4. d

Ferrell, Hirt, Bates & Currie, Business: A Changing World, First Edition

Chapter 15 Money and the Financial System

CHAPTER OUTLINE

Introduction

Money in the Financial System
       Functions of Money
       Characteristics of Money
       Types of Money

The Canadian Financial System
       The Bank of Canada
       Banking Institutions
       Nonbanking Institutions
       Electronic Banking
       Challenge and Change in the Commercial Banking Industry

CHAPTER OBJECTIVES

After reading this chapter, you should be able to:
- Define money, its functions, and its characteristics.
- Describe various types of money.
- Specify how the Bank of Canada manages the money supply and regulates the Canadian banking system.
- Compare and contrast commercial banks, savings and loan associations, credit unions, and mutual savings banks.
- Distinguish among nonbanking institutions such as insurance companies, pension funds, mutual funds, and finance companies.
- Investigate the challenges ahead for the banking industry.
- Recommend the most appropriate financial institution for a hypothetical small business.

CHAPTER RECAP

Money is the one tool used to measure personal and business income and wealth. **Finance** is the study of money: how it's made, how it's lost, and why.

MONEY IN THE FINANCIAL SYSTEM

Money is anything generally accepted in exchange for goods and services. While paper money was first used in North America in 1685 (and even earlier in Europe), the concept of fiat money--a paper money not readily convertible to a precious metal such as gold--did not gain full acceptance until the Great Depression in the 1930s.

Money serves three important functions. As a medium of exchange, money facilitates the buying and selling of goods and services and eliminates the need for bartering. As a measure

Chapter 15 Money and the Financial System

of value, it serves as a common standard or yardstick of the value of goods and services. As a store of value, it serves as a way to accumulate wealth until needed. The value of stored money is directly dependent on the health of the economy.

To be effective, money must be readily acceptable for the purchase of goods and services and for the settlement of debts. It must be easily divisible into small units of value. For money to function as a medium of exchange, it must be easily moved from one location to another. Money must be stable and maintain its declared face value. It must be durable and retain its original qualities over a long period of time and through much handling. Finally, money must be difficult to counterfeit. Every country takes steps to make counterfeiting difficult.

Many forms of money are accepted for payment or in exchange for products. A **chequing account** (also called a demand deposit) is money stored in an account at a bank or other financial institution that can be withdrawn without advance notice. One way to withdraw funds from a chequing account is by writing a cheque, a written order to a bank to pay the indicated individual or business the amount specified from money already on deposit. Cheques are legal substitutes for currency and coins and are preferred for many transactions due to their lower risk of loss. Some chequing accounts earn interest (a small percentage of the amount deposited in the account that the bank pays to the depositor). The NOW (negotiable order of withdrawal) account offered by most financial institutions is one such interest-bearing account.

Some assets are called **near money** because they are very easily turned into cash, but they cannot be used directly as a medium of exchange like paper money or cheques. The most common type of near money account, the **savings account** (also known as a time deposit), is an account with funds that usually cannot be withdrawn without advance notice (although this is seldom enforced). Savings accounts are not generally used for transactions or as a medium of exchange, but their funds can be moved to a chequing account or turned into cash. **Money market accounts** are similar to interest-bearing chequing accounts, but have more restrictions. **Certificates of deposit (CDs)** are savings accounts that guarantee a depositor a set interest rate over a specified interval of time as long as the funds are not withdrawn before the end of the interval. **Credit cards** can access preapproved lines of credit granted by a bank or company. MasterCard and Visa represent the majority of all credit cards, but American Express and cards issued by major department stores and oil company cards are also popular. A **debit card** looks like a credit card but works like a cheque. The use of a debit card results in a direct, immediate, electronic payment from the cardholder's chequing account to a merchant or other party. Other forms of near money include traveler's cheques, money orders, and cashier's cheques, which the issuing organization guarantees will be honored and exchanged for cash when presented.

THE CANADIAN FINANCIAL SYSTEM

The Canadian financial system fuels the economy by storing money, providing investment opportunities and making loans.

The guardian of the Canadian financial system is the Bank of Canada, which was founded in 1934 with the purpose of regulating credit policy and currency in the best interest of the economic life of the nation. As a crown corporation, the Bank of Canada is the sole issuer of

Chapter 15 Money and the Financial System

currency and has the authority to facilitate management of Canada's financial system. The Bank of Canada is responsible for monetary policy, central banking services, currency and administration of the public debt.

The Bank of Canada seeks to protect the value of the Canadian money by keeping inflation low and stable. It does this by controlling the supply of money available in the economy and through monetary policy.

The Bank of Canada manages the rate of growth of the money supply indirectly through its influence on the Target Overnight Rate which influences other interest rates with resulting impact on the level of spending and economic activity in the country.

When interest rates fall, individuals and businesses are apt to increase their money holdings, to borrow more and to increase spending and investment. When interest rates rise the reverse is true as fewer new loans are sought and borrowers attempt to reduce debt to avoid higher costs resulting in a slowing of the growth of money supply.

The Bank influences interest rates through its cash management activities with the objective of ensuring that short-term interest rates adjust in line with the goal of non-inflationary growth.

The Bank of Canada is also the sole issuer of Canadian bank notes and advises the government in matters relating to the public debt.

BANKING INSTITUTIONS

Banking institutions accept deposits from and make loans to individual consumers and businesses. The largest and oldest of these institutions are **chartered banks,** which perform a variety of financial services. They rely mainly on chequing and savings accounts as their major source of funds and use only a portion of these deposits to make loans to businesses and individuals. Today, banks are quite diversified and offer a number of services, including loans, credit cards and CDs, safe-deposit boxes, and trusts. **Credit unions/caisses populaires are** financial institutions owned and controlled by their depositors, who usually have a common employer, profession, trade group, or religion. Credit union members vote for directors and share in the credit union's profits in the form of higher interest rates on accounts or lower interest rates on loans.

The **Canadian Deposit Insurance Corporation (CDIC)**, established by Act of Parliament in 1967, is a Federal crown corporation. The CDIC has the responsibility of protecting the money deposited in financial institutions that are members. Under the terms of the CDIC Act, only banks, trust companies and loan companies can apply for membership. The maximum protection for each depositor with one member institution is $60,000. Although they are not eligible for membership in the CDIC, credit union deposits are similarly protected by one or more organizations in each province.

Nonbank financial institutions offer some financial services, such as short-term loans or investment products, but do not accept deposits. **Insurance companies,** for example, are businesses that protect their clients against financial losses from certain specified risks (death, injury, disability, accident, fire, theft, natural disasters) in exchange for a fee, called a premium. **Pension funds** are managed investment pools set aside by individuals, corporations, unions, and some nonprofit organizations to provide retirement income for members. Examples of pension funds include individual retirement accounts (private pension funds set up by individuals to provide for their retirement needs), corporate plans for employees, and the Canada Pension Plan (a public pension fund that collects funds from employers and employees and pays them to those eligible to receive benefits--the retired, the disabled, and young children of deceased parents). A **mutual fund** pools individual investor dollars and invests them in large numbers of well-diversified securities. A special type of mutual fund called a money market fund invests specifically in short-term debt securities issued by governments and large corporations. **Brokerage firms** buy and sell stocks, bonds, and other securities for their customers and provide other financial services. A growing number of nonfinancial firms are entering the financial arena, including manufacturing organizations, such as General Motors, that traditionally confined their financial activities to financing their customers' purchases. Additionally, **finance companies** are businesses that offer short-term loans to businesses and individuals at substantially higher rates of interest than banks. Because of the high interest rates they charge and other factors, finance companies typically are the lender of last resort for individuals and businesses whose credit limits have been exhausted and/or those with poor credit ratings.

Since the advent of the computer age, a wide range of technological innovations has made it possible to move money around the world electronically. **Electronic funds transfer (EFT)** is any movement of funds by means of an electronic terminal, telephone, or computer. Probably the most familiar form of electronic banking is the **automated banking machine (ABM)**, which dispenses cash, accepts deposits, and allows balance inquiries and cash transfers from one account to another. ABMs provide 24-hour banking services at home and abroad. **Point-of-sale (POS) systems** allow merchants to withdraw money directly from a customer's bank account the moment a purchase is made. Major banks are experimenting with **home-banking systems**.

Canadian banks currently face a rapidly changing environment with increasing competition from larger specialized financial service companies in an increasingly global market. In response to the changing environment, the federal government introduced Bill C-8 its financial sector reform legislation. The Bill provides measures that, if successful, will allow Canadian banks to better compete in this new environment and meet future challenges.

ENHANCEMENT EXRECISE

A banking system, as illustrated in the text, runs on rules and regulations. As a class or in small groups create a fictional bank. Establish rules and guidelines that must be in place for the bank to succeed. Compare the lists class-to-class or group-to-group. This exercise will give you a good idea of the thousands of rules that must be in place for a banking system to work, will illustrate the problems countries have in revamping a banking system and will also serve as a strong team building experience.

Chapter 15 Money and the Financial System

MATCHING QUIZ

Match each of the following statements with the correct key term.

a. chequing account
b. near money
c. savings account
d. money market accounts
e. certificates of deposit
f. credit cards

_____1.   This is an account with funds that usually cannot be withdrawn without advance notice.

_____2.   These are very easily turned into cash, but they cannot be used directly as a medium of exchange like paper money or cheques.

_____3.   These are similar to interest-bearing chequing accounts, but have more restrictions.

_____4.   This is money stored in an account at a bank or other financial institution that can be withdrawn without advance notice.

_____5.   These provide access to preapproved lines of credit granted by a bank or company.

_____6.   These are savings accounts that guarantee a depositor a set interest rate over a specified interval of time as long as the funds are not withdrawn before the end of the interval.

TRUE/FALSE QUIZ

Indicate whether each of the following statements is true or false.

_____1.   A chequing account is money stored in an account at a bank or other financial institution that usually cannot be withdrawn without advance notice.

_____2.   Money serves as a medium of exchange, a measure of value, and a store of value.

_____3.   The Bank of Canada can determine how large a down payment individuals and businesses must make on credit purchases of expensive items.

_____4.   Point-of-purchase systems are faster than traditional methods of payment and help reduce cheque-processing costs and hot-cheque problems for merchants.

_____5.   Only coins and paper bills can be used as money.

Chapter 15 Money and the Financial System

_____6. Near money includes time deposits, money market accounts, certificates of deposit, credit cards, traveler's cheques, money orders, and cashier's cheques.

_____7. A debit card works like a credit card.

_____8. When the economy expands too quickly, the Bank of Canada reduces the amount of money in circulation.

_____9. As a medium of exchange, money serves as a common standard of the value of all goods and services.

_____10. Certificates of deposit are similar to interest-bearing chequing accounts but have more restrictions.

_____11. Pension funds are managed investment pools set aside by individuals, corporations, unions, or nonprofit organizations.

_____12. The Bank of Canada has many shareholders.

_____13. Stability allows people who wish to postpone purchases to do so without fear that their money will decline in value.

_____14. Chartered banks in many provinces offer home equity loans, by which home owners can borrow against the appraised value of their already purchased homes.

_____15. The Canadian Pension Plan is a mutual fund.

_____16. The Bank of Canada and the Federal Reserve meet daily to control the flow of money in North America.

_____17. Monies deposited in credit unions are insured by the CDIC.

_____18. Credit Unions/caisses populaires are owned and controlled by their depositors.

_____19. Money market funds pool individual investor funds and invest them in well-diversified securities.

_____20. To remain stable and be universally accepted, money must be very difficult to counterfeit.

MULTIPLE-CHOICE QUIZ

Choose the correct answer for each of the following questions.

Ferrell, Hirt, Bates & Currie, Business: A Changing World, First Edition

Chapter 15 Money and the Financial System

_____1. Which of the following controls the money supply through the sale or purchase of government securities?
    a. monetary policy
    b. open market operations
    c. reserve requirements
    d. discount rate
    e. credit controls

_____2. The ability of a dollar bill to survive going through the washer has to do with its
    a. acceptability.
    b. divisibility.
    c. portability.
    d. stability.
    e. durability.

_____3. Which of the following functions of money eliminates the need for bartering?
    a. medium of exchange
    b. measure of value
    c. store of value
    d. acceptability
    e. divisibility

_____4. Which of the following are owned and controlled by their depositors?
    a. commercial banks
    b. savings and loan associations
    c. credit unions/caisses populaires
    d. thrifts
    e. finance companies

_____5. Which of the following are primarily concerned with the buying and selling of securities for others?
    a. insurance companies
    b. pension funds
    c. mutual funds
    d. brokerage firms
    e. finance companies

_____6. Which of the following are savings accounts that guarantee a depositor a set interest rate over a specified interval of time as long as the funds are not withdrawn early?
    a. NOW accounts
    b. money market accounts
    c. certificates of deposit
    d. money market funds
    e. time deposits

Chapter 15 Money and the Financial System

_____7.   Which of the following make loans to high-risk businesses and individuals?
       a.   finance companies
       b.   insurance companies
       c.   brokerage firms
       d.   money market funds
       e.   pension funds

_____8.   Which of the following allow(s) large companies to deposit employee paycheques directly into their employees' personal chequing accounts?
       a.   electronic funds transfer
       b.   automated banking machines
       c.   automated clearinghouses
       d.   point-of-sale systems
       e.   home banking

_____9.   Which of the following is NOT a form of near money?
       a.   credit card
       b.   chequing account
       c.   savings account
       d.   traveler's cheque
       e.   money market account

SKILL-BUILDING QUIZ

In the "Build Your Skills" exercise of your text, you researched financial service institutions in your area. Continue to build on that exercise by answering the following questions.

_____1.   You and your fiancee have determined that you will probably need 24-hour banking services for the purposes of obtaining cash and making deposits and account transfers. Which of the following would best serve your needs?
       a.   automated clearinghouse
       b.   automated banking machine
       c.   point-of-sale system
       d.   home banking system

_____2.   In considering investment opportunities for the cash you expect to receive from your parents as a wedding gift and given the fact that you have no previous investment experience, which of the following represents the safest way to invest with minimum or no risk and ability to retrieve your money on short notice?
       a.   short-term certificate of deposit
       b.   mutual fund
       c.   chartered bank money market account
       d.   all of the above

_____3.   The advantages of _____ to you and your fiancee include convenience,

Chapter 15 Money and the Financial System

safety, and potential interest earnings.
a. ABMs
b. Canadian Pension Plan
c. a credit card
d. direct deposit

ANSWERS

MATCHING QUIZ

1	2	3	4	5	6
.	.	.	.	.	.
c					
	b	d	a	f	e

TRUE/FALSE QUIZ

1. F	5. F	9. F	13. T	17. F
2. T	6. T	10. F	14. T	18. T
3. T	7. F	11. T	15. F	19. F
4. T	8. T	12. F	16. F	20. T

MULTIPLE-CHOICE QUIZ

1. b	4. c	7. a
2. e	5. d	8. c
3. a	6. c	9. b

SKILL-BUILDING QUIZ

1. b	2. d	3. d

Chapter 16 Financial Management and Securities Markets

CHAPTER OUTLINE

Introduction

Managing Current Assets and Liabilities
        Managing Current Assets
        Managing Current Liabilities

Managing Fixed Assets
        Capital Budgeting and Project Selection
        Assessing Risk
        Pricing Long-Term Money

Financing With Long-Term Liabilities
        Bonds: Corporate IOUs
        Types of Bonds

Financing With Owners' Equity

Investment Banking

The Securities Markets
        Organized Exchanges
        The Over-the-Counter Market
        Measuring Market Performance

CHAPTER OBJECTIVES

After reading this chapter, you should be able to:
- Define current assets and describe some common methods of managing them.
- Identify some sources of short-term financing (current liabilities).
- Summarize the importance of long-term assets and capital budgeting.
- Specify how companies finance their operations and fixed assets with long-term liabilities, particularly bonds.
- Discuss how corporations can use equity financing by issuing stock through an investment banker.
- Describe the various securities markets in Canada
- Critique the short-term asset and liabilities position of a small manufacturer and recommend corrective action.

Chapter 16 Financial Management and Securities Markets

CHAPTER RECAP

INTRODUCTION

Without effective management of assets, liabilities, and owners' equity, all businesses are doomed to fail. Financial management addresses issues pertaining to obtaining and managing funds and resources necessary to run a business successfully. All organizations must manage their resources effectively and efficiently if they are to achieve their objectives.

MANAGING CURRENT ASSETS AND LIABILITIES

Managing short-term assets and liabilities involves managing the current assets and liabilities on the balance sheet. **Current assets** are short-term resources such as cash, investments, accounts receivable, and inventory. **Current liabilities** are short-term debts such as accounts payable, accrued salaries, accrued taxes, and short-term bank loans. The terms *current* and *short-term* are used interchangeably because short-term assets and liabilities are usually replaced by new ones within three or four months and always within a year. Managing current assets and liabilities is sometimes called **working capital management** because short-term assets and liabilities continually flow through an organization and are thus said to be "working." The chief goal of financial managers who focus on current assets and liabilities is to maximize the return to the business on cash, temporary investments of idle cash, accounts receivable, and inventory.

A crucial element in financial management is effectively managing the firm's cash flow, the movement of money through the organization on a daily, weekly, monthly, or yearly basis. Astute money managers try to keep just enough cash on hand, called **transaction balances,** to pay bills, such as employee wages, supplies, and utilities as they fall due. To ensure that enough cash flows through the organization quickly, companies try to speed up cash collections from customers. One way to do this is to have customers send their payments to a **lockbox**, an address for receiving payments, instead of directly to the company's main address. Large firms with many stores or offices around the country can also use electronic funds transfer to speed up collections.

If cash comes in faster than it is needed to pay bills, businesses can invest the cash surplus for periods as short as one day or for as long as one year, until it is needed. Such temporary investments of cash are known as **marketable securities.** Many large companies invest idle cash in Canadian **Treasury bills (T-bills),** which are short-term debt obligations the Canadian government sells to raise money. **Commercial certificates of deposit (CDs)** are issued by commercial banks and brokerage companies. Unlike consumer CDs, which must be held until maturity, commercial CDs may be traded prior to maturity. A popular short-term investment for larger organizations is **commercial paper**--a written promise from one company to another to pay a specific amount of money. Some companies invest idle cash in international markets such as the **Eurodollar market,** a market for trading Canadian dollars in foreign countries.

Many businesses make the vast majority of their sales on credit, so managing accounts receivable is also an important task. To encourage quick payment, some businesses offer some of their customers 1 or 2 percent discounts if they pay off their balance within a specified period of time. Late payment charges of between 1 and 1.5 percent discourage slow payers. The larger the early payment discount offered, the faster customers will tend to pay their accounts; however, such discounts increase cash

Chapter 16 Financial Management and Securities Markets

flow at the expense of profitability. Balancing the added advantages of early cash receipt against the disadvantages of reduced profits is difficult, as is determining the optimal balance between the higher sales likely to result from extending credit to customers with less than perfect credit and the higher bad-debt losses likely to result from a lenient credit policy.

While the inventory that a firm holds is controlled both by production needs and marketing considerations, the financial manager has to coordinate inventory purchases to manage cash flows. The object is to minimize the firm's investment in inventory without experiencing production cutbacks due to critical materials shortfalls or lost sales due to insufficient finished goods inventories. Optimal inventory levels are determined largely by the method of production. Inventory shortages can be as much of a drag on potential profits as too much inventory.

While having extra cash on hand is positive, a temporary cash shortfall can be a crisis. There are several potential sources of short-term funds to overcome a cash crunch. The most widely used source of short-term financing, and the most important account payable, is **trade credit**--credit extended by suppliers for the purchase of their goods and services. Most trade credit agreements offer discounts to organizations that pay their bills early. Virtually all organizations obtain short-term funds from banks. In most instances, the credit services granted these firms takes the form of a fixed dollar loan or a **line of credit,** an arrangement in which a bank agrees to lend a specified amount of money to the organization upon request--provided that the bank has the required funds to make the loan. Banks also make **secured loans**--loans backed by collateral that the bank can claim if the borrower does not repay the loan--and **unsecured loans**--loans backed only by the borrower's good reputation and previous credit rating. The *principal is* the amount of money borrowed; *interest* is a percentage of the principal that the bank charges for use of its money. The **prime rate** is the interest rate banks charge their best customers (usually large corporations) for short-term loans. Additionally, most financial institutions, such as insurance companies, pension funds, money market funds, and finance companies, make short-term loans to businesses. In some instances, companies sell their accounts receivable to a finance company known as a **factor,** which gives the selling organizations cash and assumes responsibility for collecting the accounts. Additional nonbank liabilities that must be managed are taxes owed to the government and wages owed to employees.

MANAGING FIXED ASSETS

While most business failures are the result of poor short-term planning, successful ventures must also consider the long-term consequences of their actions. Managing the long-term assets and liabilities and the owners' equity portion of the balance sheet is important for the long-term health of the business. **Long-term (fixed) assets** are expected to last for many years--production facilities (plants), offices, equipment, furniture, automobiles, etc. In today's fast-paced world, companies need the most technologically advanced, modern facilities and equipment they can afford, but modern and high-tech equipment carries high price tags. Obtaining long-term financing can be challenging for even the most profitable organizations; for less successful firms, such challenges can prove nearly impossible.

The process of analyzing the business's needs and selecting the assets that will maximize its value is called **capital budgeting**, and the capital budget is the amount of money budgeted for investment in such long-term assets. All assets and projects must continually be reevaluated to ensure their compatibility with the organization's needs. If a particular asset does not live up to expectations, then management must determine why and take necessary corrective action.

Chapter 16 Financial Management and Securities Markets

Every investment carries some risk. When considering investments overseas, risk assessments must include the political climate and economic stability of a region. The longer a project or asset is expected to last, the greater its potential risk because it is hard to predict when a piece of equipment will wear out or become obsolete. The level of a project's risk is also affected by the stability and competitive nature of the marketplace and the world economy as a whole.

The ultimate profitability of any project depends not only on accurate assumptions of how much cash it will generate but also on its financing costs. Because a business must pay interest on borrowed funds, the returns from any project must cover both the costs of operating the project and the interest expenses for the debt used to finance its construction. The most efficient and profitable companies can attract the lowest-cost funds because they typically offer reasonable financial returns at low relative risks. Newer and less prosperous firms must pay higher costs to attract capital because these companies are riskier.

FINANCING WITH LONG-TERM LIABILITIES

To open a new store, build a new manufacturing facility, or research and develop a new product, companies need to raise low-cost, long-term funds. Two common choices for raising funds are attracting new owners (*equity financing*) and taking on long-term liabilities (*debt financing*). **Long-term liabilities** are debts that will be repaid over a number of years, such as long-term bank loans and bond issues. Companies may raise money by borrowing it from commercial banks or other financial institutions in the form of lines of credit, short-term loans, or long-term loans.

Aside from loans, most long-term debt takes the form of **bonds,** which are debt instruments that larger companies sell to raise long-term funds. In essence, the buyers of bonds (bondholders) loan the issuer of the bonds cash in exchange for regular interest payments until the loan is repaid on or before the specified maturity date. The bond itself is a certificate, an IOU, that represents the company's debt to the bondholder. Bonds are issued by corporations; national, province; public utilities; and nonprofit corporations.

The bond contract, or *indenture,* specifies the terms of the agreement between the bondholders and the issuing organization. It specifies the face value of the bond and its initial sales price (typically $1,000). The price of the bond on the securities market will fluctuate along with changes in the economy and in the creditworthiness of the issuer. Bondholders receive the face value of the bond along with the final interest payment on the maturity date. The indenture also specifies the coupon, or annual interest, rate, which is the guaranteed percentage of face value that the company will pay to the bond owner every year. The bond indenture may also cover repayment methods, interest payment dates, procedures to be followed in case the organization fails to make interest payments, conditions for early repayment of the bonds, and any conditions related to collateral.

There are many different types of bonds. Most bonds are **unsecured,** meaning that they are not backed by specific collateral; such bonds are termed *debentures*. **Secured bonds** are backed by specific collateral that must be forfeited in the event that the issuing firm defaults. Whether secured or unsecured, bonds may be repaid in one lump sum or with many payments spread out over a period of time. **Serial bonds** are actually a sequence of small bond issues of progressively longer maturity. The firm pays off each of the serial bonds as they mature. **Floating rate bonds** do not have fixed interest

Chapter 16 Financial Management and Securities Markets

payments; instead, the interest rate changes with current interest rates otherwise available in the economy. High-interest bonds, or **junk bonds,** offer relatively high rates of interest because they have higher inherent risks.

FINANCING WITH OWNERS' EQUITY

A second means of long-term financing is through equity. Sole proprietors and partners own all or a part of their businesses outright, and their equity includes the money and assets they have brought into their ventures. Corporate owners, however, own stock or shares of their companies, which they hope will provide them with a return on their investment. Shareholders' equity includes common stock, preferred stock, and retained earnings. Common stock, the single most important source of capital for most new companies, is often separated into two parts on the balance sheet--common stock at par and capital in excess of par. The *par value* of a stock is the dollar amount printed on the stock certificate and has no relation to actual *market value*--the price at which the common stock is currently trading. The difference between a stock's par value and its offering price is called *capital in excess of par.* Preferred stock is corporate ownership that gives the shareholder preference in the distribution of the company's profits, but not the voting and control rights accorded to common shareholders.

When a corporation has profits left over after paying all of its expenses and taxes, it can retain all or a portion of its earnings and/or pay them out to its shareholders in the form of dividends. **Retained earnings** are reinvested in the assets of the firm and belong to the owners in the form of equity. Retained earnings are an important source of funds and are, in fact, the only long-term funds that the company can generate internally. When a corporation distributes some of its profits to the owners, it issues them as cash dividend payments. Not all firms pay dividends. The **payout ratio**--dividends per share divided by earnings per share--expresses the percentage of earnings the company paid out in dividends.

INVESTMENT BANKING

A company that needs more money may be able to obtain financing by issuing stock. **Investment banking,** the sale of stocks and bonds for corporations, helps companies raise funds by matching people and institutions with money to invest with corporations in need of resources to exploit new opportunities. The first-time sale of stocks and bonds directly to the public is called a *new issue.* When a company offers stock to the public for the very first time, it is said to be "going public," and the sale is called an *initial public offering.* New issues of stocks and bonds are sold directly to the public and to institutions in what is known as the **primary market**--the market where firms raise financial capital. The primary market differs from **secondary markets,** which are stock exchanges and over-the-counter markets where investors can trade their securities with others. Corporations usually employ an investment banking firm to help sell their securities in the primary market. An investment banker helps firms establish appropriate offering prices for their securities and takes care of the many details and securities regulations involved in the sale of securities.

THE SECURITIES MARKETS

Securities markets provide a mechanism for buying and selling securities. They make it possible for owners to sell their stocks and bonds to other investors, so they may be thought of as providers of

Chapter 16 Financial Management and Securities Markets

liquidity--the ability to turn security holdings into cash quickly and at minimal expense and effort. Unlike the primary market in which corporations sell stocks directly to the public, secondary markets permit the trading of previously issued securities. There are many different secondary markets for both stocks and bonds. It is the active buying and selling by many thousands of investors that establishes the prices of all financial securities. **Organized exchanges** are central locations where investors buy and sell securities. Buyers and sellers are not actually present on the floor of the exchange, but are represented by brokers, who act as agents and buy and sell securities according to investors' wishes. The **over-the-counter (OTC) market** is a network of dealers all over the country linked by computers, telephones, and teletype machines.

Performance measures--averages and indexes--help investors and professional money managers determine how well their investments performed relative to the market as a whole, and they help financial managers determine how their companies' securities performed relative to that of their competitors. Averages and indexes not only indicate the performance of a particular securities market, but provide a measure of the overall health of the economy. An *index* compares current stock prices with those in a specified base period, such as 1944, 1967, or 1977. An *average* is an average of certain stock prices. Some stock market averages are weighted averages, where the weights employed are the total market values of each stock in the index. Many investors follow the activity of the Toronto Stock Exchange Index in Canada or the Dow Jones Industrial Average in the United States to see whether the stock market has gone up or down. A period of large increases in stock prices is known as a *bull market,* with the bull symbolizing an aggressive, charging market and rising stock prices. A declining stock market is known as a *bear market,* with the bear symbolizing a sluggish, retreating market. When stock prices decline very rapidly, the market is said to *crash.*

ENHANCEMENT EXERCISE

Individually or in small groups, select ten stocks that trade on any North American market and track the results for one month. Compare which stocks performed better and then compare the results to the indexes in general.

MATCHING QUIZ

Match the following statements with the correct key term.

a. bonds
b. unsecured bonds
c. secured bonds
d. serial bonds
e. floating rate bonds
f. junk bonds

_____1.   These bonds are not backed by specific collateral.

_____2.   This is a sequence of small bond issues of progressively longer maturity.

_____3.   These are debt instruments that larger companies sell to raise long-term funds.

Chapter 16 Financial Management and Securities Markets

_____4.   These bonds are backed by specific collateral that must be forfeited in the event that the issuing firm defaults.

_____5.   These bonds do not have fixed interest payments; instead, the interest rate changes with current interest rates otherwise available in the economy.

_____6.   These bonds offer relatively high rates of interest because they have higher inherent risks.

TRUE/FALSE QUIZ

Indicate whether each of the following statements is true or false.

_____1.   Discounts offered to credit customers get cash flowing through the firm faster and increase profitability.

_____2.   Trade credit is an arrangement by which a bank agrees to lend a specified amount of money to an organization upon request.

_____3.   The Dow Jones Average is weighted by price.

_____4.   The par value of a stock is the price at which it is currently trading on the securities market.

_____5.   Bonds are issued only by corporations.

_____6.   Capital budgeting is the process of analyzing the needs of the business and selecting the assets that will maximize its value.

_____7.   Trade terms of "1/10 net 30" mean that a business may take a 1 percent discount if it makes payment by the tenth day after receiving the bill; otherwise, it must pay the whole amount within 30 days.

_____8.   Retained earnings are distributed to a company's owners in the form of dividends.

_____9.   More profitable businesses can attract lower-cost financing for the purchase of assets than can newer or less profitable companies.

_____10.   Historically, junk bonds have been associated with companies in poor financial health and/or start-up firms with limited track records.

_____11.   Secured loans are backed by the borrower's name and good reputation.

_____12.   If a bond quote gives a coupon rate of 8 3/8 on a $1,000 bond, the bond owner will receive $83.75 in annual interest for that bond.

Ferrell, Hirt, Bates & Currie, Business: A Changing World, First Edition

Chapter 16 Financial Management and Securities Markets

_____13. Lockboxes allow a business to have access to payments made by customers more quickly than if the payments were sent directly to the company.

_____14. A new issue is the sale of the first shares of stock ever issued by a particular company.

_____15. The longer the expected life of an asset, the less is its potential risk.

_____16. Factors purchase other companies' accounts receivable.

_____17. Commercial paper is issued by commercial banks and brokerage companies.

_____18. Securities markets provide liquidity.

_____19. Primary markets are the markets where publicly owned securities are traded.

_____20. Optimal inventory levels are determined largely by the method of production.

MULTIPLE-CHOICE QUIZ

Choose the correct answer for each of the following questions.

_____1. Which of the following is a debt obligation of the government?
   a. accounts receivable
   b. commercial paper
   c. Eurodollar market
   d. Treasury bill
   e. certificate of deposit

_____2. Which of the following is a sequence of small bond issues of progressively longer maturity?
   a. junk bonds
   b. floating rate bonds
   c. serial bonds
   d. secured bonds
   e. unsecured bonds

Chapter 16 Financial Management and Securities Markets

_____3.   Which of the following is a percentage of the loaned amount that a bank charges to use its money for a given length of time?
   a. prime rate
   b. security
   c. principal
   d. collateral
   e. interest

_____4.   Which of the following is NOT a current asset?
   a. cash
   b. marketable securities
   c. accounts payable
   d. accounts receivable
   e. inventory

_____5.   The dollar amount printed on a stock certificate is the stock's
   a. coupon rate.
   b. capital in excess of par.
   c. market value.
   d. par value.
   e. dividend yield.

_____6.   Which of the following is NOT an example of debt financing?
   a. common stock
   b. debenture
   c. 30-year bank loan
   d. junk bond
   e. serial bond

_____7.   Which of the following compares current stock prices with those in a specified base period?
   a. index
   b. average
   c. bull market
   d. bear market
   e. crash

_____8.   Which of the following trades most corporate bonds and all government securities?
   a. Midwest Stock Exchange
   b. over-the-counter market
   c. New York Stock Exchange
   d. Toronto Stock Exchange
   e. Pacific Coast Exchange

Ferrell, Hirt, Bates & Currie, Business: A Changing World, First Edition

Chapter 16 Financial Management and Securities Markets

_____9.   Which of the following has the lowest risk?
   a.   expansion into new markets
   b.   repair of old machinery
   c.   introduction of a new product into foreign markets
   d.   purchase of new equipment for an established market
   e.   introduction of a new product into a familiar market

_____10.   Which of the following allows a business to have faster access to payments made by customers?
   a.   Canada Post
   b.   electronic funds transfer
   c.   marketable securities
   d.   safe deposit boxes
   e.   lockboxes

_____11.   Production facilities, offices, and equipment are examples of
   a.   current liabilities.
   b.   fixed liabilities.
   c.   current assets.
   d.   fixed assets.
   e.   working capital items.

_____12.   A factor makes a profit by buying other companies'
   a.   products.
   b.   accounts payable.
   c.   accounts receivable.
   d.   transaction balances.
   e.   certificates of deposit.

_____13.   Which of the following is a marketable security arising from international trade?
   a.   certificate of deposit
   b.   Eurodollar market
   c.   commercial paper
   d.   T-bills
   e.   bank loans

_____14.   Which of the following is where stocks and bonds are sold directly to the public and to institutions?
   a.   primary market
   b.   secondary markets
   c.   tertiary markets
   d.   securities markets
   e.   over-the-counter market

Chapter 16 Financial Management and Securities Markets

_____15.   Which of the following is NOT a current liability?
    a. accounts payable
    b. notes payable
    c. wages payable
    d. inventory
    e. taxes payable

SKILL-BUILDING QUIZ

In the "Build Your Skills" exercise you practiced assessing risk on six projects. Continue that exercise by answering the following.

_____1.   Which of the following should be considered for project 2 (Brazilian government)?
    a. political climate
    b. economic stability
    c. competitive nature of the marketplace
    d. all of the above

_____2.   Which of the following would carry the lowest risk?
    a. expand into a new market
    b. buy new equipment for an established market
    c. introduce a new product in a familiar area
    d. add to a produce line

_____3.   Which of the following projects would have the greatest potential risk?
    a. one that is expected to last 10 years
    b. one that is expected to last 5 years
    c. one that is expected to last 1 year
    d. one that is expected to last 6 months

ANSWERS

MATCHING QUIZ

1. b   2. d   3. a   4. c   5. e   6. f

Ferrell, Hirt, Bates & Currie, Business: A Changing World, First Edition

Chapter 16 Financial Management and Securities Markets

TRUE/FALSE QUIZ

1. F	5. F	9. T	13. T	17. F
2. F	6. T	10. T	14. F	18. T
3. T	7. T	11. F	15. F	19. F
4. F	8. F	12. T	16. T	20. T

MULTIPLE-CHOICE QUIZ

1. d	4. c	7. a	10. e	13. b
2. c	5. d	8. b	11. d	14. a
3. e	6. a	9. b	12. c	15. d

SKILL-BUILDING QUIZ

1. d	2. b	3. a